Your People *Are* Your Product

Your People *Are* Your Product

How to Hire the Best So You Can Stay the Best

Don Blohowiak

Chandler House Press
Worcester, Massachusetts

Your People Are *Your Product:*
How to Hire the Best So You Can Stay the Best

Copyright © 1998 by Don Blohowiak

All rights reserved. Printed in the United States of America. No part of this book may be used or reproduced, stored or transmitted in any manner whatsoever without written permission from the Publisher, except in the case of brief quotations embodied in critical articles and reviews.

ISBN 1-886284-10-5
Library of Congress Catalog Card Number 97-77507
First Edition
ABCDEFGHIJK

Published by
Chandler House Press
335 Chandler Street
Worcester, MA 01602 USA

President
Lawrence J. Abramoff

Publisher/Editor-in-Chief
Richard J. Staron

Vice President of Sales
Irene S. Bergman

Editorial/Production Manager
Jennifer J. Goguen

Book Design and Production
CWL Publishing Enterprises
3010 Irvington Way
Madison, WI 53713 USA
www.execpc.com/cwlpubent

Cover Design
Marshall Henrichs

Chandler House Press books are available at special discounts for bulk purchases. For more information about how to arrange such purchases, please contact Irene Bergman at Chandler House Press, 335 Chandler Street, Worcester, MA 01602, or call (800) 642-6657, or fax (508) 756-9425, or find us on the World Wide Web at www.tatnuck.com.

Lead Well and Natural Selection Hiring Method are trademarks of the author.

Chandler House Press books are distributed to the trade by
National Book Network, Inc.
4720 Boston Way
Lanham, MD 20706
(800) 462-6420

Contents

Preface	ix
Part One. Rethinking "Hiring"	1
Chapter One. Retrofit or Better Fit?	3
Human Retrofitting	5
High Stakes Hiring	8
What You Take for Granted Still Costs You	9
Hire Productivity	10
Without Method or Reason	12
Rethinking Hiring: The Natural Selection Hiring Method™	15
Chapter Two. Who Is "Qualified"?	19
In Search of Competence	24
Exclusionary Rules: Minimum Qualifications	28
Credentials—Credible?	32
Chapter Three. Personality Is Competence	39
Personal Considerations	42
Fit for Duty	50
Feels Like Home	52

vi   Contents

Part Two. The Natural Selection Hiring Method™   55

Chapter Four. Define the Job to Define Who You Hire   57
    The Nature of a Job   59
    Does Anybody Really Know What Job It Is?   61
    Profiling a Given Job   65
    Rating the Human Components   70
    Performance Domains and Capacities for Work   72
    Putting It All Together   87
    Essentials   87

Chapter Five. Predicting the Future by Sitting in Judgment   91
    Probing Questions   93
    Reliably Invalidating Validity   94
    Judgment and Designer-Label Bias   96
    The Curse of the Knowing Eye   99
    Assortment of Assessments   101

Chapter Six. Assessing Applicants: A Process   113
    Defining the Desirable   115
    Creating the Key Qualifications Profile   117
    Tracking Candidate Assessments   122
    Scoring: Many Are Called, Few Are Chosen   128

Chapter Seven. This Is a Test... This Is *Only* a Test   131
    G and the Search for Intelligent Life   143
    Test Mart   147
    Validity and Correlation: Freudian Slips?   149

Chapter Eight. Interviewing: "So, Tell Me about Myself"   153
    For Sale: Applicant, Mint Condition; Ready, Willing, and Able   154
    Can You Recall a Time When You Asked a Question?   155

Beyond Behavioral and Scenario Interviews	159
Values at Work	163
Valuing Applicants	165
Getting to the Tarnish Beneath That Shine	171
Grounding Candidates with "Levelers"	173
Interviews: Valid and Reliable?	174
The Interview Process	180
Great Beginnings and Endings	182

Part Three. Other Important Information for Employment Deployment — **187**

Chapter Nine. Staying Out of Hiring Manager's Prison: Legalities — **189**
Key Do's and Don'ts	192
About Disabilities	193

Chapter Ten. Long-Term Relationships: Recruiting and Retention — **195**
Magnet Recruiting	197
Luring the Fish from the Sea	198
Retain the Gain: Keep What You Recruit	205

Appendix. Attributes of Corporate Culture — **208**

Index — **215**

Preface

> New opinions are always suspected, and usually opposed, without any other reason but because they are not already common.
>
> –John Locke
> 1690

Hiring rates as the most overlooked and undervalued component of effective leadership. On its surface, hiring (including internal promotions and reassignments) appears resoundingly pedestrian—a mundane, routine activity repeated unceremoniously thousands of times a day in the business world. In common practice, the task amounts to an apparently simplistic exercise: finding someone with adequate skills, having them fill out a withholding tax form, and putting them right to work. In other words, insert candidate A into open position B.

> The all-too-common reality, in far too many companies, is that hiring processes are poorly designed and shabbily executed.
>
> –Fast Company magazine

As a management concept, hiring certainly doesn't sound nearly as seductive as strategic visioning, or as intriguing as *workforce engagement*, or as captivating as *creating the learning organization* or any of the other faddish notions that routinely sweep through Corporate America's collective consciousness. Still, after working with a wide variety of large and small enterprises in North America and abroad, I've reached a conclusion that is not commonly voiced in business and management literature. With capital, technology, and information now universally and easily available to all competitors, the dominant determinant of success in today's intensely competitive business world is—without question—this: Shrewdly selecting people to do work that productively takes full advantage of their individuality and unique competencies.

"Productivity is the true competitive advantage," declares the dean of management thinking, Peter Drucker. In an economy predicated on knowledge and service, productivity is decidedly dependent on people—especially having the right people in the right jobs. Sustained competitiveness and profitability are inextricably tied to selecting—purposefully, intelligently, and methodically—the people who make up an organization. This should be an intuitively obvious truism that's instantly appreciated by anyone who has suffered "help" by a surly sales clerk, or who was forced to return to the garage—for a second or third time—a car that was supposedly repaired. And it should be equally clear to any manager who tries all the pop management techniques but still can't seem to get her charges to meet ambitious but reasonable goals.

Careful selection of employees—with their very individual skills, behaviors, beliefs, attitudes and needs—*matters*. It always has. But it matters more now than ever before. The quality of an organization's innovation, the level of caring service that it provides to its customers, and its capacity to respond quickly to a changing environment are all the direct products of exclusively human competencies. And they can vary markedly from human to human. (As we shall see later, there are many, many competencies—some apparent, some invisible—that an organization could require from its employees. Companies must both clearly identify those attributes and carefully screen to find people who embody them. And then, after acquiring them, work to keep them on the payroll.)

Choosing the people who collectively make up a company is a responsibility without equal. Yet, employee selection is surrounded by myths, folk remedies, and, it seems, everyone's "secret recipe" for hiring. Relying on habitual, anecdotal, or homespun methods is increasingly dangerous from both a competitive perspective and a legal standpoint. In the face of a tight labor market (that demographers say isn't going away anytime soon), and a fiercely competitive global marketplace, increasingly more value is going to be placed on the one attribute of an organization that cannot be replicated by a competitor: a company's unique workforce composed of unique people. On the legal front, the courts are facing a swell of employment related suits. It is a growth industry for lawyers. Government agencies and jurists alike are demanding accountability for the specific methods by which firms attract, select, and promote their employees.

To better understand the commonplace but extraordinarily important activity of hiring, I examined the available—and surprisingly sparse and hard to come by—literature on it. So much of it was fragmented and disjointed ("ten million questions you possibly could ask job applicants"). Or dense, turgid prose ("the philosophic, theoretic, and empirical underpinnings of pre-employment testing subjected to meta-analytic scrutiny employing multivariate regression with varimax rotation dwelling on t- z- and *trailing p* scores of comparative stanines and eigenvalue plots contrasted with orthoblique item-scale linkages and monotonic multidimensional scaling with multiple chi-squared communalities and common factor coefficients to elicit methodological artifacts"). Or collections of mere anecdotal musings ("there's a guy in Omaha who tests the mettle of job applicants using a barrage of stress tactics").

I reviewed 25 years worth of studies by industrial psychologists (many now prefer the term "organizational psychologist") on job analysis and hiring selection methodologies. Their conclusions?

- General intelligence tests do predict job performance. And they don't. Or they do but with adverse impact on people in protected classes.
- Complex job analysis data gathering processes do accurately assess the knowledge, skills, abilities, and other characteristics, a person needs for a given job. Or, those complicated, highly specialized procedures may overstate—and/or understate—important task, cognitive, and personality-related aspects of the job.
- Personality tests are a better assessment device than those that test for general intelligence (what psychologists call g, lay people call IQ, and critics call discriminatorily narrow, academic-achievement-in-the-dominant-culture predictors). Or, personality assessments are an irrelevant, inaccurate, violating invasion of a person's most private self.
- Assessment Centers (work simulations designed, observed, and monitored by specially trained professionals) accurately predict an individual's future job success and promotability. Or they are artificial, sterile, contrived and unrealistic (not to mention quite expensive) environments in which skilled people can appear incompetent, and lesser lights can brightly shine.
- Pre-employment tests can be proven to be both valid and reliable. But the validity is often false, contorted, or marginal, and therefore the reliability is meaningless.
- Employment interviews (the requisite rite of passage—or rejection—deployed in frequency without equal by apparently *every* hiring manager in the Western world) can rival the best-written assessment instruments in predicting a candidate's future job performance. And they can yield so many useful insights about the applicant that no mere test ever could. Or, the traditional job interview rates as the worst method for screening people. It is not only unreliable in predicting job performance, it fails to assess competencies, reveal shortcomings, and worse, it is notorious for denying job opportunities to otherwise capable people who happen to be in protected classes.

What's a concerned (and understandably confused) businessperson to do? Clearly, there is a need for an effective, practical process—a *system*—that managers can deploy to discharge their most vitally important responsibility: Choosing the people who will determine the fate of the organization. Such a system would treat hiring holistically—defining the critical outcomes and competencies of a given job, redefining job descriptions, re-thinking the meaning of "qualified," and redesigning the selection process (which, even for many experienced managers, is too often a disorganized, inconsistent, chaotic and ineffective ad hoc eruption of unguided, time-wasting activity).

So here, in this volume, is that practical system—the *Natural Selection Hiring Method*™—that an individual manager can put to work in virtually any organization. If yours has sophisticated Human Resource professionals available to assist you, so much the better. But, even with no HR assistance, most any manager with a modest investment of thought and time can effectively put the Natural Selection Hiring Method to work selecting people who will work more competently, more productively, and more happily.

After you've put the Natural Selection Hiring Method to work, I'd very much appreciate your feedback on how the system works for you, the modifications you made to it, and the innovations you created for it. Please send your comments to one of the addresses below.

Thank you for hiring me to assist you in this important work.

Don Blohowiak
Lead Well Development
Box 791
Princeton Jct., NJ 08550-0791

DonB@LeadWell.com
www.LeadWell.com

ACKNOWLEDGMENTS

With profound gratitude to...

Bill Harned	Clint Ober	John Schaller
Paul Krejci	Jim Birmingham	Tom Jonas
Bill Moos	Tom Hauff	Tony Rizzo
George Otwell	Jay Bowles	Roy Steinfort
Greg Groce	Al Brauer	Pam Sallander
Jeff Krames	Cindy Zigmund	Ron Fry
Janet Pickover	Brian Palmer	Susan Ullrich
Capps B. Sutherland		

...who hired for competence and potential, not qualifications

Many thanks to the thoughtful people who helped to inform my thinking by spending time with me and sharing their ideas and materials with me, especially Herbert Greenberg, Lynne Pou, Alan Davidson, Terri Kabachnick, Ann Rhoades, James Farr, Lee Bowes, Bob Losyk, and members of the Tri-State Human Resources Association.

Dick Staron of Chandler House Press gave me the instant green light to pursue this project and I am extremely grateful for his faith in the concept and his endurance awaiting its completion. John Woods of CWL Publishing Enterprises helped to translate raw material into what you see here.

And a special note regarding my indebtedness to my partner Susan Blohowiak. She provided many insights, resources I never would have otherwise come across, and selflessly helped in more ways than I can recount or ever repay. She bravely blew the whistle when this work was off-track in its early iterations and patiently helped to reorient it. I am so glad she did.

I take responsibility for what's here, with the full knowledge of how much less it would have been without the assistance of these kind people.

–Don Blohowiak

Part One
Rethinking "Hiring"

Chapter One
Retrofit or Better Fit?

Chapter Two
Who Is "Qualified"?

Chapter Three
Personality Is Competence

Chapter One

Retrofit or Better Fit?

If "how knowledge" were easily transmitted and quickly imitated, mastering the art of building committed and productive workforces would not provide any competitive advantage.

–Jeffrey Pfeffer
Stanford Graduate School of Business

The elements of good business management have all become quite familiar (if not universally adopted): total quality management, employee empowerment, continuous process improvement, teamwork, and myriad other developments. Now, the battle for a competitive edge in the marketplace must be fought on a new front: selecting your workforce.

Knowledge and service—provided by your company's employees—power your company's competitive position. **Your employees are the product you're selling to your customers**.

This fundamental truth holds not only for firms selling services but is equally true in manufacturing companies. Today, they increasingly depend on:

- the knowledge and skill of employees working with so-

phisticated technology on the assembly line (increasingly, employees simply support the technology that does the actual manufacturing),
- the imagination of the people who design and promote market-beating products, and
- the service expertise and personality of the many people who will interact with customers by selling and supporting the manufactured products in the brutally competitive marketplace.

> Today, people have to be more than an asset. They are the company.
> –Gerald Greenwald
> Chairman, CEO, United Airlines

With such great dependence on your human assets, your firm's capacity to compete successfully likely hinges on some frustratingly elusive qualities in your employees:

- the depth of their intelligence (which can be far more than the classic definition of verbal and mathematical ability),
- the breadth of their imagination,
- the intensity of their commitment to customer satisfaction,
- their capacity to learn (and unlearn) ideas and methods,
- their propensity to adapt, and
- their capability to continue producing greatness amid turmoil—all the while absorbing increasingly greater expectations, shaking off disappointments, and continually confronting soul-numbing change.

How does one manage *that*? The first part of the answer: *from the beginning*. You had better start early, because the financial stakes are enormous.

Back in 1981, an article appeared in *American Psychologist* about better hiring and its effect on productivity. Frank L. Schmidt of the U.S. Office of Personnel Management and George Washington University, and his co-author John E. Hunter of Michigan State University, wrote that they "calculate the gross national product would be increased by $80 to $100 billion per year if improved [employee] selection procedures were introduced throughout the economy."

Now, even using the late senator Everett Dirksen's old

standard ("a billion here, a billion there, and pretty soon you're talking about real money"), that figure is astounding. And if you were to factor in the inflation during the years since the article appeared, the number might even make the former senator from Illinois sit up and take notice.

Admittedly, Schmidt and Hunter arrived at their figure using some fancy mathematical extrapolations predicated on a broad set of assumptions. Still, gains from better hiring do add up in the real world. In retailing, known for its low pay and high turnover, the fully-loaded cost of replacing a full-time employee can run to $10,000; replacing managers who defect can cost three times that, according to figures gathered by Kabachnick and Company, a Connecticut-based management consulting firm specializing in the retail industry. Employee turnover in retail stores often runs at 90% a year. One retailing firm that Kabachnick worked with had an average annual employee turnover of 85%. After helping the company to institute employee-screening procedures to better match employees with jobs more suited to their personalities by using behavioral and values assessments (discussed in greater detail in Chapter 7), that annual turnover figure plummeted from 85% to 23%. "Naturally," says company president Terri Kabachnick with a great deal of understatement, "the client was pleased with the results and realized a substantial improvement in its cost structure."

HUMAN RETROFITTING

Why does employee selection make a great financial impact? It's all about productivity. Consider all the management wisdom you've digested over the years from books, conferences and formal coursework. When you distill it, most management advice condenses into this: exhortations to change your company by *retrofitting* your employees.

Working to reshape, recast, or reform people who, for whatever reason, are either ill-suited to your corporate culture or who are basically in the wrong jobs is a time-consuming, frustrating, and essentially futile effort. By contrast, when you have the right people in the right jobs, you need to spend far less time struggling with human retrofitting—hollow, vain efforts to make employees something they're not.

The futility of human retrofitting is magnified by a startling realization: *The vast majority of people are employed in positions for which they are personally not well-suited.* Herbert M. Greenberg, widely published on hiring matters and president of employment testing and human resource consulting firm Caliper, Inc., suggests that research consistently bears out that about 80% of employees hold a job that is not appropriate for their individual interests and behavioral preferences.

> You can tinker with products to improve them, but people aren't so easily changed.
> –Lee Bowes
> Author, CEO of America Works, Inc.

The crucial implication in Greenberg's finding is this: When you rely on past experience as the critical screen for hiring new talent, you may actually *increase* your odds of hiring a misfit. Think of it this way: If four out of five people hold a job for which they are not truly well suited, and you are selecting your applicants from a pool of people with prior work experience in the job you're filling, then you have an 80% chance of hiring someone you probably shouldn't. By hiring—or promoting—someone because of his or her work experience, you may perpetuate the mismatch and harm your organization by obtaining less productivity than if you had made a better hire.

For example, take the case of someone who has an accounting degree and ten years of experience in tax accounting. As a job applicant, she obviously possesses the work experience and technical skill to fill the vacancy for a state sales tax specialist in your accounting department. After all, she is, in the classic (but obsolete) sense, "qualified." But not obvious to you (and probably not even to her), she secretly hates all the solitary research and detail work; she really craves social interaction. After the euphoria of the new assignment begins to fade, she's going to be miserable and under-productive in that tax accountant job. That not-so-apparent mismatch could cost her peace of mind, and cost you—her unsuspecting employer—precious productivity. You'll lose efficiency through the accountant's lost time—time spent away from doing undesirable detail work, time spent correcting errors, and even increased time away from work for sick leave.

The importance of this *misemployed* concept is further heightened when you consider internal promotions. If you are promoting from a basically misaligned labor pool, you likely will select only the "least worst" and have the inadequate leading the inappropriate.

Miscast and Misaligned

Management consulting firm Kabachnick and Company studied approximately 1,600 retail workers at all levels. Using a variety of assessment instruments, the employees were profiled for their behavioral preferences, attitudes, values and beliefs, as well as their perceptions of the skills their jobs required. Major finding: 62% of the frontline employees did not have the personal attributes to be effective in their customer service and sales positions. (To validate this study, simply walk into your average retail establishment and do your own quick assessment of employee attitudes.)

Furthermore, in the management ranks, Kabachnick found that many managers had a difficult time motivating their charges because the boss's personal behavioral orientation was more task-oriented than people-oriented. "Top management set objectives for getting the work done through teamwork," explains Terri Kabachnick, "but middle and frontline managers were oriented to working alone. Or they managed with an attitude toward 'developing' teams of 'tell 'em what to do and they should do it.' It's no wonder turnover in the industry averages a staggering 90% a year."

Both productivity and employee retention improve, Kabachnick says, when there is a better match between job and employee. "People aligned with their jobs produce better. The key is to 'define and align.'"

HIGH STAKES HIRING

In today's leaner organizations, every position counts more. This magnifies the potential financial impact of every position on the payroll—in terms of potential positive contribution to revenue and earnings, or, conversely, of costs and losses.

When you hire well, you benefit from internally motivated employees who like their work and want to excel at it. Employees who fit well with their jobs and with their employing organization are lower-maintenance. Their error rates are lower, and so is their absenteeism and turnover. Their tenures are longer, their morale higher. If you've taken the time and made the effort to screen well from a reasonably good candidate pool, your new hires are more likely to be both brilliant and resilient in a turbulent, changing environment. In short, well-chosen employees are more productive. And, with fewer "people problems," so are you. Figure 1-1 summarizes this point.

> A recent report from Ernst & Young says that institutional investors are now more likely to buy stock based on a company's ability to attract talented people.
> —Fortune
> January 12, 1998

On the other side of the ledger, the financial impact of a bad hiring decision can be calculated in numerous costs:

- recurring recruiting expenses wasted on washouts;
- managerial time squandered on reviewing résumés and interviewing candidates;
- training and orientation time and expense entirely lost upon employee departure;
- management time spent correcting, counseling, and cajoling a poor performer; and

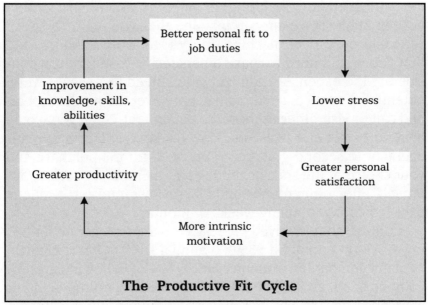

Figure 1-1. Employees who are better suited to their jobs work better and live more happily.

- lost productivity (and missed opportunities) while the poor hire was under-performing.
- lost sales and profits from customers driven away by mis-hires;

Some costs persist even if the position is vacant:

- lost productivity by other employees who suffered a drag on their morale, or perhaps were even driven away by mis-hires (especially bad hires in the management ranks); and
- legal expenses (and, potentially, damage award payments) for truly bad decisions in the hiring process.

WHAT YOU TAKE FOR GRANTED STILL COSTS YOU

Despite the financial stakes, organizations often approach hiring too casually. By comparison to, say, authorizing major capital expenditures, hiring is often a downright loosey-goosey affair. For example, imagine that you want to spend $125,000 on a new machine, the Widget 2098. Chances are that you would need to make a persuasive case for even considering the expense. Then you would need to review several potential vendors of similar units, pore over the product specs, and call or visit other users of the equipment. Then you would have to empanel a task force, involve several layers of management to second-guess both the need for the purchase and your choice of the specific model, and then obtain several approvals after numerous rounds of reviews and justifications over the course of many weeks or months.

Contrast that involved process with the typical one for hiring a person earning a $35,000 annual salary—not a big deal in many companies. You interview a few of the candidates for an hour or so, invite one or two back for a follow-up, and ask your boss and maybe a colleague to spend another fifteen minutes or so verifying your impressions. Then you go ahead, committing the corporation to a likely outlay of well over $125,000.

Over $125,000? The math is simple. If the new hire stays just three years, you're paying $105,000 even without a penny's raise. Plus, with benefits averaging about a third of salary these days, you're tacking on an additional $11,550 a year for nearly another $35,000, plus training, plus equipment and supplies... That "no big deal" $35,000 hire turns out to be a decision worth about $150,000.

HIRE PRODUCTIVITY

Selecting people well-suited to their work boosts productivity twice: first, in every job that is performed better; and second, in freeing managerial time to be spent on activities that add more value than wrestling with the workforce. People well suited to their positions and the culture of their employer need less supervision, do higher-quality work, and are more productive than people who intend well but are mismatched to their duties and place of employment.

People who love their work because they are well matched to it are motivated by their work. They don't require pep talks, threats, complex review systems, convoluted incentive programs, or many of the endless variations on the theme of human retrofitting in the workplace.

> Getting the right mixture of people seems to be 80 percent of success, and the other 20 percent is just not getting in their way.
> –Scott Adams
> Creator of Dilbert

More than ever before, as official statistics bear out, tenure for virtually everyone in a given job is growing shorter and shorter. If someone hasn't been downsized and outplaced, they've been restructured and reassigned. The result is more churning on the payroll than ever before. And because internal reassignments often involve qualification assessments and evaluations, managers are making more hiring decisions more often. They need to be sure those critical decisions are not only not willy-nilly nor helter-skelter but rather the best they can be.

Hiring is not merely a necessary chore to complete in order to fill open slots in the organization chart. Hiring will account for how well a company stacks up competitively and how well it performs financially. Simply put, hiring ranks as the most important determinant of success in today's brutally competitive world. Just try to imagine being the market leader with a slow, unimaginative, and uncommitted workforce—the kind that haphazard hiring may very well put on your payroll.

> Let's face it, half the people are below average in the world. You just have to be a fanatic about hiring good people.
> –Esther Dyson
> Computer Industry Analyst

Employees who are best suited to their jobs and the organization that employs them produce better results than those less well suited. With pressure to produce goods and services in faster cycle times, to compete on the quality of an organization's customer service, and to draw profits from greater efficiency rather than premium prices, the performance of every individual in every job counts more. An organization that has not maximized the contribution from every person in every position suffers from organizational drag that keeps it from soaring.

WITHOUT METHOD OR REASON

All this points to one of the great mysteries of the business world. The very managers who are absolutely convinced that their company's fate rests in the hands of employees—"our most important asset," they'll call them—are often uninformed, casual, and inconsistent in the way they select those employees. In fairness, it may well be that they simply do not know better. Hiring, as a topic of executive and managerial import, has been resoundingly ignored.

A recent review of the course catalogs from major management education institutions such as the American Management Association, the Wharton School's Executive Education Program, and the Conference Board, amazingly, showed no focus on hiring. There was no shortage of seminars on global marketing, finance management, quality programs, customer service, and the like. But one would be hard pressed to find curricula on the vitally important competency of selecting the people who would hold the fates of their employers in their heads and hands. Wharton's ten-day course on "The Essentials of Management" promises sessions on global perspective; innovation, technology and learning; thinking strategically; and, yes, managing people. But the catalog says nothing about selecting people.

A training course that the American Management Association describes as one of its "best sellers" purports to improve "Managerial Skills of the New or Prospective Manager." The course, offered more than a hundred times yearly at numerous locations throughout the country (at a cost of well over $1,000 per attendee), claims to teach nascent managers how to dele-

Retrofit or Better Fit? 13

gate to employees, motivate employees, coach employees, and conduct employee evaluations. But nary a word is said about effectively selecting those employees to whom one would delegate and whom one would motivate and evaluate. It is, in a word, all about retrofitting—a terribly limiting concept to indoctrinate new managers into, but one that, sadly, owes its unfortunate heritage to a long tradition of managers selecting their colleagues haphazardly and inadequately.

In fairness, the AMA catalog does offer a course of instruction on employee selection buried within its section aimed at human resource professionals. But most hiring decisions are made by operating managers who arguably aren't searching for expertise in information aimed at the human resources function. (Even in AMA's course catalog index that lone "recruiting and interviewing" seminar course is cataloged as a subset of "human resources." There is no index entry for "hiring.")

Furthermore, of the many business conferences I attend (and, as a keynote speaker on leadership and productivity, I attend scores a year), virtually none treat employee selection as a featured topic. Sure, there's an occasional breakout session on hiring. But usually its scope is extremely limited and non-strategic, covering narrow topics such as complying with the Americans with Disabilities Act or "Questions You Should Never Ask an Applicant Unless You Want to Get Sued." These offerings typically come from an "employment lawyer" who has never hired anyone in his life.

> When employees are promoted to managerial positions, they are ordained with certain managerial powers. One of these is the power to make hiring decisions. Unfortunately, this power comes sans the knowledge or training on how to do it.
> –Richard J. Pinsker
> Pinsker and Company

Stalwart management education organizations simply ignore hiring as an essential managerial competency. So is it surprising that generations of managers have bumbled through their hiring by simply relying on prejudice ("You can usually tell if you're going to hire someone in the first five minutes of meeting them"), instinct ("I know a winner when I see one"), and misinformation ("We couldn't possibly afford to hire someone who doesn't have experience in performing this job")?

Or is it any wonder that managerial mythology confuses most managers by embracing competing truths: Employment tests do and don't help you select applicants better; stress interview techniques do and don't help you identify people who have the constitution to work in a fast-paced environment; and selecting applicants based on their personal "chemistry" does and doesn't help assure a good fit with the organization? The unfortunate fact is that most managers rely on their GUT for selecting their hires from available applicants (GUT, of course, being an acronym for Guess und Try 'em).

In conclusion, hiring as a strategic responsibility and tutored discipline appears to be lost to most managers who need it most. This is potentially tragic. In the service and knowledge economy—where success is wholly dependent on the humanity comprising the organization's payroll—hiring must rank as a key *strategic* imperative. Surely, some people in the human resources camp understand this. But most operating executives don't operate as though *they* do. Hiring expertise is grossly undervalued as a key managerial competency.

Companies large and small have examined and refined their processes for marketing, manufacturing, distribution, accounting, and information acquisition and retrieval. Now, everyone must rein in and replace the reckless process by which people are invited to join a payroll (or change their role on one).

> Everything has changed, except the way we think.
> –Albert Einstein

Rethinking Hiring: The Natural Selection Hiring Method™

Most professional advice on hiring, even that found in the few books addressing this vital topic, tends to be incomplete, fragmented, or both. However, this book takes an unusually holistic approach. Getting a superior match between job applicants and the work you would hire them to do takes more than merely asking clever interview questions. It is a *process* (Figure 1-2). This book takes you through that process. It provides operating managers—the ones who do the actual hiring—with the necessary thinking, tools and processes to accomplish this important work. You'll find a method that is more reliable and more consistent with hiring's increasing strategic stature than the patchwork of conflicting and fragmented advice and procedures so often associated with the topic of hiring.

An important principle underlying the hiring process described in this work is this: People who do work they enjoy and to which they are personally well adapted will do it better (quality), longer (productivity), and with greater joy (morale and service).

The Natural Selection Hiring Method described in this book includes useful processes for clarifying what work you really need done, identifying the personal characteristics requisite for accomplishing the work objectives, and attracting qualified candidates to do that work well. It advises you on how to pierce the blue-suited armor of the many sound-alike—and often well-coached and well-rehearsed—job candidates in order to reach and reveal the real person with whom you might have to spend your professional life (most of your waking hours). It also helps you sift through the available candidates to narrow your selection options.

> Selection [typically] is not treated as an integral process that can otherwise contribute to productivity.
>
> –Susan Sturm and Lani Guinier
> California Law Review, July 1996

This book gives you both a conceptual foundation and a structural framework to take the guesswork out of the hiring process, and provides you with the information and tools you need to make and keep that perfect hire. You'll likely need all the information and tools you can get. The task in hiring is literally to predict the future. As you assess the person you are about to hire, you are literally predicting the future fortunes of the individual and, in turn, your company.

16 Your People *Are* Your Product

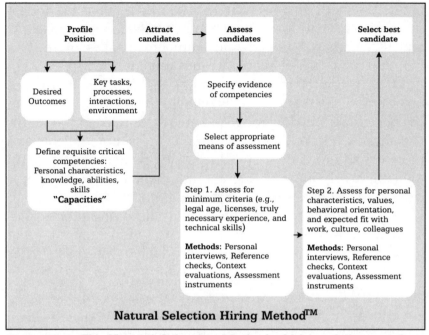

Figure 1-2. The Natural Selection Method of hiring follows a clear process to help you assess the kind of employee you need to accomplish your objectives, and identify people who bring the required competencies to the work.

Timely Advice

Early in my business career, I worked on the 20th floor of an office building in downtown Detroit that housed both of Michigan's largest utilities, Michigan Bell and Detroit Edison. One day, while riding the elevator down to the lobby, I overheard two very frustrated colleagues commiserating. I'm not sure which utility company employed them, but I suspect that their comments could have applied to either one. Either way, their brief conversation has stuck with me for some twenty years:

Employee 1: "I can't believe it!"
Employee 2: "Yeah. Incredible."
Employee 1: "After all that rushing around and all that hard work!"

Retrofit or Better Fit?   17

Employee 2: "Why is it that we never have time to do it right, but we always have time to do it over again?"

That simple and profound sentiment has rung in my ears many times since I first heard it on the elevator that day. Sure, it's a common cliché, but that doesn't make it invalid. And the idea certainly applies to hiring. Let's be clear: Using the Natural Selection Method will take more time than hiring willy-nilly. At least, your investment of time at the front end of the hiring process will be greater

> Instead of saying, "But we don't have enough time!" we must ask, "How are we going to deploy the limited time we have so that we can make our work truly effective?"
> –Grant Wiggins

than it probably is right now. But you should get a very good return on your investment.

Every moment you spend recruiting, screening, and assessing a more appropriate hire is a moment you get back several fold (perhaps hundreds and thousands of times over) by not having to spend your precious moments monitoring, correcting, hand-holding, and the like. Without question, you will spend untold additional hours of supervisory time with (or because of) a less appropriate or inappropriate hire.

There's a concept in manufacturing that's applicable to all work: scrap and rework. Anything that's wasted—including and perhaps especially time, which cannot be salvaged, reused or recycled—is scrap, an unnecessary expense and drain on profitability. Rework—doing the same task over again (and maybe yet again)—wastefully burns time and robs you of productivity. Anything that keeps you and your colleagues from delivering great work quickly and efficiently, such as

> A decline from superior to average performance may not be as visible as a decline from average to poor performance, but it can be just as costly in terms of lost productivity.
> –Frank L. Schmidt and John E. Hunter

an unproductive or incompetent employee, steals from you and your firm.

Time is a finite, precious, non-renewable resource. You must invest it wisely, guard it jealously, and protect it vigorously. The time you take to hire well is multiplied miraculously.

Not investing the necessary time to hire well is like not investing your money and then wondering why you never have more of it. A wise investment of time, like money, yields increasing dividends over time. Don't you think it's about time to get the productivity advantage that comes with a truly productive staff? That's an idea whose time has clearly come.

Chapter Two

Who Is "Qualified"?

> We live in a time perhaps for the first time in our history where experience may be a detriment.
> —Food Services Logistics Executive

Competency in our fast-changing world is not what someone already knows and what they've done in the past. Rather, competency today is what someone can imagine, what they are capable of learning, and willing to try. These qualities are more difficult to assess, but to dismiss them because they are not blatantly self-apparent, don't leap out from a résumé, and do not fit neatly into a little box on an application for employment is organizationally self-destructive folly.

The basic premise that underlies most hiring (and even much of the advice in books, articles, and seminars about hiring, even if it's held out as cutting-edge) is a faulty one. The premise is that prior experience *qualifies* one for a seemingly similar post. Assuming that someone who has training in a field or even prior experience in it is suitable to engage in it is an extremely limiting view of qualification for a position. It is the *skill-fill fallacy*—the mistaken idea that a job should be held by someone assumed to have adequate skills because they previously filled a similar-sounding job. Job experience means one has held a position and been charged with completing tasks. It says nothing of accomplishment, productivity, or even anything about having any real interest in the work, much less a knack for it. Such deficiencies violate the very concept of being *qualified*.

The word *qualified* literally means (and has since the 16th century) to possess or be endowed with attributes that would make one fit for a certain purpose. When we say one is qualified for a task, we declare that they are capable of accomplishing it, and we predict their success in undertaking and completing it. But in another sense, the word can mean something a bit different. Think about a time you were asked to answer a question with yes or no and felt uncomfortable with such a blanket declaration. You may have replied, "First, let me *qualify* my response..." When someone says that, they intend to restrict in some way what they're about to say.

In the same sense, when we seek people who are *qualified*, we limit or restrict the applicant pool to those we presume will be successful in completing the task at hand. The point of division is between those who are in the limited group for consideration, usually because they did similar work in the past, and those who are restricted from demonstrating—or acquiring—the capability because they don't have the exclusive prerequisite, which may be wholly irrelevant to performance potential.

Competent but Not Qualified

People with the requisite technical skills and even necessary personal attributes are occasionally prohibited from providing those services to an employer by the employer's institutionalized biases. Clearly there is much concern in our society over denying employment opportunities to members of minority groups. But there are more subtle forms of qualification discrimination.

Who Is "Qualified"?

The entertainment conglomerate founded by Walt Disney considers all its employees to be "Cast members," as if every employee belonged to a cast of characters in one grand, non-stop production. In a 1997 article profiling Disney's renowned service quality, Quality Digest, a magazine for quality professionals, observed, "Nonconformists needn't apply [to Disney]. For example, male cast members are prohibited from wearing earrings or having facial hair."

What role are the men of Disney supposed to be playing? Why does the corporate script prohibit this modicum of personal expression? Does a mustache infringe on a man's capacity to do a competent job? Did it undermine the credibility of Walter Cronkite, Mahatma Gandhi, or Martin Luther King, Jr.? Does an earring in either a woman's or a man's ear prevent responsive customer service or any other competent execution of duty? (Disney won't comment on the company's hiring practices. A spokesman said flatly, "It serves no corporate purpose to do so." Ironically, a week after hitting the brick wall with Disney's public relations department, I received a promotional flyer from the company offering to share its management secrets with other businesspeople. Right there on the agenda: hiring practices. The seminar cost just under $3,000 per person. Now that serves the corporate purpose.)

I have my own bias. I, too, think facial hair is offensive—when it's not groomed. I have worn a neat, closely clipped beard for more than five years. As someone who is hired many times a month—as a management conference speaker I'm hired by scores of companies every year—I know that some people will not hire me because I have a beard (as did Abe Lincoln, Charles Darwin, Ernest Hemingway, Alexander Graham Bell, Henry David Thoreau, Charles Dickens, Robert Reich, Luciano Pavarotti, Sigmund Freud, George Bernard Shaw, Louis Pasteur, Jesus...). I am happy to say that I am happy not to work for a company that would not hire me because I have a beard. I prefer to work with people of broader intellect.

22   Your People *Are* Your Product

Now let's talk about you. Do you want to eat in a restaurant where you're served by unmistakably unattractive people? Is "presentableness" a valid job criterion for a fine dining restaurant? For a diner? Why? Is an experienced, friendly, attentive yet grossly overweight server with crooked teeth who is perspiring competent? Is this question different than asking, "If customers in a small Southern town say they would be 'offended' by table service provided by a black waiter, and would refuse to patronize a restaurant that hires any, is it OK not to hire any?"

Qualified and competent aren't always visible to the unaided eye even when they seem to be—and hiring issues are never simple.

Work in most organizations increasingly means more interacting with team members and pleasing customers (both internal and external), and less division of labor and less isolation and specialization of tasks. In this context, being qualified takes on a much broader sense than having a degree or certification in a subject (which probably represents outdated knowledge the day it is conferred in our rapidly changing world). It certainly means more than having performed a task in the past, even for decades. Many of the factors that contribute to an organization's success cannot be represented in a job's list of tasks or shown on a process flowchart.

> What is qualified? What have I ever been qualified for in my life? I haven't been qualified to be a mayor. I'm not qualified to be a songwriter. I'm not qualified to be a TV producer. I'm not qualified to be a successful businessman. And so, I don't know what qualified means. And I think people get hung up on that in a way, you know?
>
> —Sonny Bono, U.S. Congressman, former mayor of Palm Springs, CA, songwriter of ten gold records, producer of popular TV shows, and successful restaurateur, quoted by the Los Angeles Times in 1992

Consider the following examples:

- Initiative
- Commitment to quality
- Empathy for others
- Willingness to endure imperfect conditions and produce good work anyway
- Resilience in the face of setbacks
- Responsiveness to changing circumstances
- Selfless cooperation with colleagues
- Dedication to the needs of customers
- Mature judgment
- Deference to deadlines
- Emotional stability
- Perseverance to complete difficult tasks
- Reliability

Ever try to glean these essential qualities, and many other important ones, from a résumé? In terms of their contribution-to delivering a successful performance, how important are these human attributes (so-called *soft skills*)? Most managers, in a reflective moment, consider them to be somewhere from 50% to 85% of the success equation. So why don't hiring managers try to assess for them? Why don't most hiring discussions even mention them? Because the invisible is easy to overlook, and the difficult-to-measure is easy to dismiss. But that doesn't make them affect success any less.

Equally Qualified?

Occasionally, I hear managers comment about their struggle to decide between two "equally qualified" job applicants. Or I'll read a news report about some well-meaning government agency or civil rights group charging that a potential employer subjected one of two "equally qualified" candidates to unfair discrimination in the hiring process.

No doubt, unfortunately, there are some hiring managers who discriminate unfairly based on irrelevant qualities such as race, age, religion, or other factors. Arguably, they are inflicting harm not only on the individual denied a professional opportunity but also to their employer. How? By denying the organization access to potentially its most productive employee, whose employment prospects they have dismissed prematurely, prejudicially, and irrationally. Still, the concept of equally qualified is mostly an imaginary one. Qualified implies a qualitative judgment, which is not and cannot be precise or absolute.

Even identical twins with the exact same education and work experience are probably not equally qualified for a given position. Each individual has a uniquely different orientation to life and work (more patient/less patient, more decisive/less decisive, more outgoing/more reserved, and a thousand other distinctions) that makes one more likely to be suited for success in a given job or specific work environment than the other.

The task before a hiring manager is to clearly identify and assess the relevant factors that will contribute to probable success in a particular job—topics undertaken throughout this book. In most cases, the real success factors for top performance in a position are going to include a mix of knowledge, demonstrable skills, work or life experience, and personality elements. Given all the variables, it's extremely unlikely that any two applicants for a specific post in a particular firm at any given time are going to be equal.

IN SEARCH OF COMPETENCE

We need to get past the limiting concept of qualified, which is restricted to those presumed to have a capability because they are believed to have done something similar in the past. Instead of qualified, we should think in terms of competent (Figure 2-1).

The word *competence* comes from the same Latin root from which we derive *compete* and *competition*. If, at first glance, be-

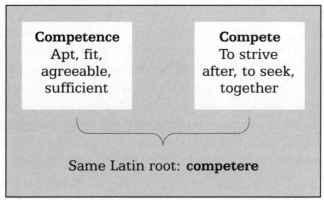

Figure 2-1. The ability to compete effectively is directly tied to your organization's competence.

ing competent and engaging in competition seem like unrelated qualities, a quick look back at the words' common origin reveals some intriguing wisdom for contemporary managers striving to hire people in order to compete in the modern marketplace. The early meaning of *competent* was "apt, fit, agreeable, and sufficient." To *compete* originally meant "strive after, to seek together." So, taking a cue from the ancients, if you want to have an organization that can compete effectively today, you need sufficiently fit, agreeable people striving together.

This idea of *fit* is paramount. How well an individual fits into his or her work assignment—how emotionally comfortable with it he or she feels—is not a matter of self-indulgence. On the contrary. Given the increasing degree of intellectual contribution, autonomy or interaction with colleagues and customers, as well as the independent decision-making that is expected from people in nearly every occupation, how people *feel* about their work has a direct bearing on both their productivity and the quality of work they produce.

Individuals' fit with their work extends beyond their personal interest in, and affinity for, a position's tasks and duties. Fit includes the unique aspects of the organization in which they perform those duties, the people they work with day-to-day, the physical environment, the pace of performing, and so on. Their appropriateness for a job extends well beyond their technical training, work experience, and even their accomplishments in the field.

An example of that comes quickly to the fore in a team environment. When work is to be accomplished through teamwork, technical qualification is only part of one's competence. For the qualification to be put to work, for it to have any value, there must be competence in the *process*. The very nature of effective teamwork depends on the synergy effect. That is, the team can meet high productivity demands because its capabilities exceed the sum of the members' individual competence.

Members of a team work differently than individuals who essentially do their work by themselves in proximity to their colleagues. Anyone who has ever been part of a group that "clicked" knows this instinctively. Teams that do not function in an effective, high-output mode are usually only work groups that have one or more members who lack either technical or team skill competence, or both. Having even outstanding technical qualifications without team competencies may render someone effectively incompetent in a true team environment.

"Team competencies" largely depend on interpersonal skills and personal attributes such as willingly trusting colleagues and sharing information; freely contributing ideas; supporting

---

Lights, Camera, Competence!

Indulge in a light-hearted fantasy illustrating a serious reality. Let's say you are casting for a role in a movie. What qualifies an actor to get the job? Is it years of related professional experience? Perhaps. Is it having a college degree or graduate degree in theatre arts? Perhaps. Is it being the subject of positive media reviews from prior acting jobs? Perhaps. Is it belonging to the Actors Guild? Perhaps. Is it sterling references from people whose reputations you know and respect? Perhaps.

In your role as casting director, you receive a résumé from none other than Arnold Schwarzenegger. You're thrilled! This guy is Mr. Boxoffice. Everyone pays to see

Who Is "Qualified"? 27

him. His movies rake in revenues in the hundreds of millions of dollars. He's accomplished. Disciplined. He is a well-rounded human being who not only is good at his craft, but also is an accomplished businessperson with wide-ranging interests. An immigrant to the United States, he has a broad, diverse, multicultural world view. He is a good guy who does ample charitable and civic work (not to mention his political connections that go straight to the White House).

Charming, well liked, he takes direction well, and has a range that spans action adventure to romantic comedy, and he plays well opposite children—he has even given birth (with a little help from special effects). He's fit, healthy as a horse, and strong like a bull. Good news: he's read the script, loves it, and wants in on this. He's available. He's even willing to forgo his fee and take a small percentage of any after-tax profits generated by the production (this is fiction, remember).

You hear from the star just in time. The one part not cast, the one opening you have, is the most critical one. Fortunately, it's for the lead, and Arnie is no stranger to anchoring movies with his star power. There's just one tiny catch. The part is that of a nine-year-old girl growing up on a ranch in Armadillo Junction, nestled in the rugged Chisos Mountains of Southwest Texas, with her lonely, widowed, paralyzed-after-an-accident mom (played nearly convincingly by Oprah Winfrey).

A true pro with a fantastic mental attitude and never-say-die spirit, Arnie persists. Against your better judgment, he talks you into an audition. He looks pretty in his little pink dress and dreadlocks. He mugs, he pouts, he suppresses his Austrian roots and gets the West Texas twang down perfectly. The wizards in makeup have given him a soft, innocent, natural, no-makeup look. Arnold Schwarzenegger, a superstar who wants to work for you, becomes a nine-year-old girl. Amazing. Virtually convincing. Almost able to pull it off. Still, no camera angle, no supercomputer-driven digitally enhanced retouching can convincingly transform that three-time title-winning Mr.

Universe bodybuilder's hulk into the little-girl frame of our heroine.

All the managerial retrofitting, training, coaching, feedback, incentives, and performance reviews in the world could not possibly alter what is fundamentally a bad fit between a specific work assignment in a given situation and someone with impressive, appropriate, and directly related work credentials. By every measure, the actor is qualified to deliver a stellar performance; he's just not competent to do this job.

---

teammates by taking on unassigned duties for "the good of the team"; sharing credit, rewards, and responsibility; and so on. While some such attributes can be broken into skill sets, many of them reflect aspects of personality (no training course will alter the true nature of someone unwilling to selflessly share information, no matter how many ways you show him how to do it). The next chapter takes a detailed look at these very personal and individual components of competence.

EXCLUSIONARY RULES: MINIMUM QUALIFICATIONS

Consider a more common, and very serious, scenario from the workaday world. Take the case of a police officer. What qualifies an applicant? By what measure can one determine who is likely to be a good police officer? People holding the job of police officer must be prepared to intervene between sparring spouses, apprehend substance-abusing reckless drivers, defuse heated disputes between differing parties, complete paperwork promptly and properly, give accurate testimony in court, understand the law, keenly observe human behavior, patiently endure verbal abuse, coax recollections from shaken witnesses, judiciously apply physical interventions, and execute many other varied responsibilities.

So what competencies must a person embody to even be considered for such a post? A few spring immediately to mind: mature judgment, strong interpersonal skills, physical stamina, listening skills, patience, and reasoning ability. But rather than seeking those qualities as a primary qualification, some states and municipalities apply a surrogate screen by requiring applicants seeking to be police officers to have a four-year college degree. Why?

The link is not obvious. Perhaps when responding to a 911 call for a burglary, the officer ought to contemplate issues given rise by having taken Philosophy 101: Are the victims predestined to suffer the loss? Was it the will of God? Is there a God? Will the suffering be rewarded in some karmic way? Should the loss be viewed as a gift—a divine endowment from which one derives appreciation for blessings otherwise taken for granted? Aren't material possessions a diminution, or enslavement, of the human spirit? Isn't private ownership only an illusion? Should we define our worth by the number of things we own?

Or perhaps that college pedigree is better applied by the officer tapping his or her reservoir of sophisticated knowledge from required college courses to draw out a suspect under arrest. They could discuss the differing properties of metamorphic or igneous rocks, or perhaps contrast the social developments of ancient China and, say, Greece. Or the merits of self-determinism in former colonial baronies ill-prepared for self-rule.

To effectively develop the skills to relate to the vast majority of citizens in the community—most of whom do not have a four-year college degree—just how valuable is the knowledge gained by absorbing a whole panoply of unrelated facts and theories that don't even pretend to have a remote application to daily life? Certainly, a future police candidate, while sitting contemplatively for four years at a school desk, develops the higher-order skills of learning how to predict what the professor will put on the exam and how to fashion essay answers exactly the way the professor wants them. Are such skills applicable to interviewing witnesses, writing traffic accident reports, tackling suspects, or comforting victims? What is it about enduring four years of chalk talks and completing a battery of fill-in-the-blank tests that is magically applicable to the rigorously physical, intensely social, and emotionally taxing work of police officers?

This is not to suggest that a four-year college education is not worthwhile, or that aspiring police officers should not seek one. The point is to question why it even remotely should screen out otherwise smart, dedicated, and caring people who might make great police officers even though they did not find the abstractions of a mandatory college curriculum appealing, could not afford the costs in dollars and time commitments, did not accumulate sufficiently good grades in high school when they were less serious about mature matters, or for whatever other reason did not acquire a four-year degree.

Now, if potential police recruits were required to have taken and passed courses on, say, investigative procedures, interpersonal communication, the varying social norms of minority communities, or succinct report writing, those might be valid screening devices. But should someone who has a degree in astronomy or art history or political science be deemed absolutely more qualified than someone who does not but grew up in the community, literally speaks its language, and cares deeply for it?

Having a college degree shouldn't be presumed to make one even minimally qualified to be considered for a position as a police officer, and not having one should not bar one from consideration. The same can be said for so-called intelligence tests. The late David C. McClelland, of Harvard, made the case vividly back in 1971 in a public lecture given at the Educational Testing Service in Princeton, New Jersey (adapted for *American Psychologist*, January 1973).

> Suppose you are a ghetto resident in the Roxbury section of Boston. To qualify for being a policeman you have to take a three-hour-long general intelligence test in which you must know the meaning of words like "quell," "pyromaniac," and "lexicon." If you do not know enough of those words or cannot play analogy games with them, you do not

qualify and must be satisfied with some such job as being a janitor for which an "intelligence" test is not required yet by the Massachusetts Civil Service Commission. You, not unreasonably, feel angry, upset, and unsuccessful. Because you do not know the words, you are considered to have low intelligence, and since you consequently have to take a low-status job and are unhappy, you contribute to the celebrated correlations of low intelligence with low occupational status and poor adjustment.

Since McClelland made his case, numerous other studies have positively correlated high scores on general intelligence tests (which tend to measure schoolwork-related skills in the verbal- and mathematical-thinking domains) with positive work performance. In other words, people who do well on such tests, the research shows, tend to do well in many work situations. But, and this is key to hiring managers, what you don't know is who you've *screened out* by using the IQ-type test. In a labor market flooded with college-educated applicants, managers can require degrees with no apparent penalty. But in a tight labor market, the degree hurdle eliminates people who otherwise might have the requisite skills to take your customers' orders, process forms, and even manage corporate colleagues. Many successful people in our culture—including Bill Gates, Peter Jennings, and Albert Einstein, to name a few—wouldn't *qualify* to manage some fast-food restaurants because they never completed college.

A related point: Some of the studies that establish the *correlation* (social scientists rarely claim to "prove" anything; they know better) between high scores on intelligence tests and work performance use supervisory ratings as the job-related success measure. Anyone who has ever been subjected to an annual performance review (the "yearly sneak attack") knows that they are imprecise, inconsistent, and often totally divorced from actual proficiency in performing work. Even when they are administered fairly—meaning there is no intentional slighting of the person being reviewed—they are subject to considerable inaccuracy and subtle bias.

For example, re-read that last sentence. It says, "... slighting of the person being reviewed." It does not say, "slighting of the work performed by the particular individual." If you caught that, give yourself a positive affirmation. The unfortunate fact is that many "performance reviews" are more like "person reviews." That's where ratings correlating alleged intelligence and alleged performance can get messy. It's no psychological revelation to report that people tend to hold other people whom they perceive to be like themselves in higher regard than people they don't identify with.

It could well be that college-educated supervisors recognize more of themselves in other people who also happen to have had the college experience. As every article in every psychology journal inevitably concludes, more research will need to be conducted on this important subject before any definitive conclusions can be drawn.

CREDENTIALS—CREDIBLE?

Conclusions about qualifications and competence often are drawn when a candidate possesses credentials—a license, certification, or earned designation. In a society drowning in verbose, hyperbolic, and inflated advertising claims, people seek to establish credibility for their claims of qualification through "credentials." (Credentials comes from the Latin *credentia*, meaning belief; people presenting credentials offer a sign that their professional expertise can be believed.)

Lawyers have credentials—a law degree and a passing score on the bar exam. Doctors have credentials—a medical degree and passing score on board exams for their specialty. Public school teachers have credentials in the form of their state teaching license. A certified public accountant has passed a state's examination for his field of knowledge, as have an architect and a professional engineer. Stockbrokers need a federal license, real estate agents and barbers are required to hold a state license. Insurance salespeople may hold the designation of Chartered Life Underwriter. Financial planners may have certifications issued by a national association, but then again, they may not.

Toiling in a line of work that's unlicensed, unregulated? Not to worry. You can have credentials, too. Just as trade unions have long tested and labeled the technical competence of their members (novice, apprentice, journeyman, master), many corporate trade and professional associations are providing their members with credentials by issuing self-styled designations and certifications. The Institute of Management Consultants, for example, confers a Certified Management Consultant title to its members who pass a written test on ethics and a verbal exam by three experienced peers. Meeting Professionals International offers a Certified Meeting Professional (CMP) designation to members who pass a written examination requiring several hours to complete. The speakers appearing at conferences organized by those meeting planners may earn a Certified Speaking Professional (CSP) designation from the National Speakers Association. The CSP can be earned after speaking (for fees) for at least three years, serving scores of clients, presenting testimonial letters from satisfied customers, and earning an average of no less than $50,000 a year in speaking fees. (Insert obvious joke about "talk's not cheap" here.)

Individual companies are also issuing "credentials" to their own salespeople in the form of "certifications" for this or that aspect of a product line. While a review of the applicable literature reveals no conferring body for Certified Rehabilitated Male (listens to women without interrupting, frequently quotes John Gray on Venusian needs and Martian shortcomings), this and other such credentials can't be far behind. The mania over credentials and certifications has reached a level some consider certifiably insane.

In some lines of work, employment may be limited to people who hold a certain credential. But credentials may be no assurance of competence. To repeat: Just because employment candidates are qualified doesn't mean they're competent. Be as rigorous or more rigorous in your review of candidates holding professional licenses or impressive-sounding but unfamiliar designations. Many professional credentials stem from a written examination—the replay of information.

Knowing a subject thoroughly doesn't make one a high achiever in it. To wit: Most business professors likely *know* much more about business than most executives; still, not too many corporate boards of directors in charge of hiring CEOs hand the reins to b-school academics. A very real example of this was reported by *Inc.* magazine when it profiled the wife of Peter Drucker, the octogenarian management theorist. She is a budding entrepreneur involved in manufacturing a small electronic timing device. When asked about the help she receives from her husband in running her company, she laughed and said the good professor doesn't know the first thing about actually running an operation such as hers.

Even many corporate managers today, as a result of downsizings and restructurings, don't fully understand some of the operations and technical functions for which they are held responsible. Their span of control has grown wider than their capacity to absorb all the nuances. Other managers put more emphasis on process and ample trust in their colleagues, giving them responsibility for staying current with and applying specialized technical expertise. As former Wharton professor Russell L. Ackoff observes, "In 1900 more than 90% of the work force could not perform their job better than their bosses could; today more than 90% can."

Competence, with or without credentialed qualifications, exists on multiple levels:

- having an interest in a type of work;
- knowing something (to everything) about a type of work;
- knowing what to do;
- being capable of doing it (which can vary considerably by degree);
- being willing to do it;
- doing it;

Who Is "Qualified"? 35

- doing it well as a matter of course;
- doing it while adapting to changing circumstances;
- doing it amid adversity;
- doing it continually better by improving knowledge, method, and output.

When hiring people, whether or not they bear credentials, having a clear sense of where their qualifications lie on this scale can help you distinguish one candidate from another and set your expectations for initial productivity and future skill development. (There's much more on this in Chapter 7 on assessing competence and performance.)

The Competence of Potential

Seeing competence as including potential is extremely liberating; it is the opposite of the tight confines imposed by the restrictions of qualified. Viewing prospective hires as people with certain dispositions, inclinations, and potential opens a much wider field of candidates to you than a narrow approach of "What have you done already?"

Some consulting firms, PR agencies, and smaller businesses hire bright people for their brains and disposition and develop the specific technical competence through training (much of which may consist of training on the job through close supervision or pairing with a mentoring colleague). A prestigious firm such as Andersen Consulting carefully recruits talented, smart young people right out of college. Unlike some other prestigious consulting firms that stalk the Ivy League business schools to cherry-pick the latest crop of MBAs, Andersen hires recent college grads. They know that the intellect in a good analytic mind, even if it was most recently studying Russian literature, can be successfully applied to clients' business problems when coupled with a

> It's not important what a person has done, but crucial where they can take the enterprise!
> –Carlos A. Webster

strong method of problem discovery and analysis. They take those fertile, energetic young minds out to the market to solve the problems of companies that perhaps were not so careful in their hiring and developing.

Many times in my own career, I have been hired for jobs that, without question, I was not qualified for. Courageous people with an eye for potential have offered me positions that even I would not have hired me for, and encouraged me when I clearly was reluctant to step out onto the high wire with inadequate education or preparation.

I recall vividly a conversation over my first business lunch. It was with George Otwell, a regional sales executive with the Associated Press ("the world's largest news-gathering organization"). George, based in Atlanta, was on a talent hunt, recruiting. We'd never met before, but he received my name from Tony Rizzo, a colleague in Washington, DC. Tony and I met briefly a few months earlier at a conference. He remembered me. Months later, when the company had an opening, Tony and George talked about me, and set out to recruit me.

Over his iced tea, George asked the 22-year-old "me" to fly, at the company's expense, from my hometown of Milwaukee (the confines of which I'd barely been outside of) to interview with some of the AP's top executives in New York City, which, in my schema of things, was just west of the moon. I was visibly unsure.

"Don, I understand your reservation. I'm offering you an opportunity to do something now that you're going to do anyway in five years," George confidently told me. He was talking about moving to the business end of the operation, selling. I was, and had always envisioned myself, on the hallowed side of the news industry, gathering news. Well, actually, I was working in local TV news at the time and there truly was nothing either journalistic or hallowed about it. But the thought of the new job, selling, was instinctually repulsive.

Still, I was intrigued. My fiancée Susan and I were to be married in just a few months. If the company offered me the job, I'd be immediately relocated to Detroit.

I went to New York. They offered me twice my current salary (which, in truth, as is commonly the case in entry-level journalism jobs, was at about poverty level), a company car, an expense account, plus commissions, plus some modest financial help with the move. I went to Detroit. Later, I was promoted to a supervisory role in Denver.

There are two lessons about my initial entry into the business world. Lesson one: Always be recruiting. George got my name from Tony, who had kept it for months. When Tony and I met casually at that conference, we did not talk about career opportunities with his company. Tony did not mention recruiting. I did not solicit a job and did not send a résumé. In fact, truth be told, I'd completely forgotten about the brief conversation until I got that exploratory call out of the blue from George.

Lesson two: Take chances. Hire potential. Seek competencies before qualifications. I did well at the company (once I made peace with the transition into sales), won awards, sold lots of business, and served my customers very well. They even wrote the company management to tell them that. I wasn't the best sales rep in the company, but I was a good one who worked hard, added value, and never forgot the faith, confidence, and responsibility (millions in annual revenue from hundreds of customer relationships) given to me when even I simply could not have justified it. (Not only had I not done the work before, I wasn't even a very good dresser. George Otwell's first investment in my career development was to hand me a copy of John T. Molloy's classic fashion advisory, *Dress for Success*. Then he told me to ditch the brown shoes for black wingtips. I had to ask him, "What are wingtips?")

After I left (five years later, again recruited for another job for which I was not "qualified"), the company paid every cent I'd earned in bonuses, and then called years later wanting to know if I had any interest in returning.

That recruiting and hiring strategy worked out well for all. But I still shake my head when I think of that episode twenty years ago. There simply wasn't any way for the company to be sure that, as a new hire, I rated as even a reasonably good risk. Oh, they did have me complete some standard written assessments, and they did interview me thoroughly. More on both in the chapters covering assessing competency.

In my own management career, I've tried to repay the favor extended to me in some small way by extending it to others. The debt remains largely unpaid. If only everyone carried such a debt. What a more committed, invigorating, and creative place we would all work in.

Chapter Three

Personality Is Competence

> Chances are, most employees you've fired were let go because of laziness, insubordination or the inability to get along with other people. Wouldn't it have been better to know ahead of time whether or not those employees had the right personalities for the job?
> –Shari Caudron
> Workforce, August 1997

We've all seen them. The sales representative who isn't the least bit persuasive, the checkout clerk who can't seem to add two and two, the teacher who appears not to like children, the receptionist who is brusque, or the manager who talks about teamwork but does little but bark orders to the other teammates. We scratch our heads and wonder, *Why would anyone hire someone like that?* Why, indeed?

Actually, the answer is usually pretty simple: Someone had a position to fill, and applicants with the "right" credentials presented themselves (and in some cases, breathing unassisted qualifies). Because they professed an interest in working for the firm to which they applied, and perhaps possessed a skill, a degree or license, or had some related experience, and, most important of all, they were willing to take the job—they were hired. As we saw in the previous chapter, those are truly inadequate reasons for hiring a job candidate.

We are all much more than the job description for our most recently held post or even the sum of all our work experiences and technical skills.

Recall that startling insight from chapter one: The vast majority of us—something along the order of 80%—may hold jobs for which we really aren't personally suited. Assume for a moment that most misemployed people have appropriate training (a big assumption) and that many have significant experience in their field (perhaps even decades' worth). That doesn't mean that they enjoy their work or consistently do well at it, or even ever do well at it. You may have had the experience of working with someone who apparently had the requisite credentials, maybe even the perfect résumé, for a job that they just weren't any good at.

People are not their résumés. They are complex, emotional creatures who vary considerably in their stamina, commitment to work, service ethic, preferences for social interaction, pace of work, attention to detail, deference to policy, interest in improving their skills, capacity for stress, inclination to be decisive, and on and on. Intuitively, we all know this. But for some reason, many managers seeking to fill an open position act as though none of this personality stuff matters. Yet it matters greatly to productivity and to the stress levels around the workplace (for the individual employee as well as his or her colleagues and perhaps customers). It also matters as to whether a manager must initiate futile human retrofitting attempts, and perhaps ultimately "build the file" to separate an individual from his or her current livelihood.

What Is a Résumé?

In my seminars, I often pose, with no set-up to skew the responses, a simple question to the participants: What is a résumé? Almost without exception, the answers that instantly fly back at me with passion and even anger are words like "fiction," "half-truths," "fantasies," "fraud," and so on. Some refer to them as propaganda, advertising, sales pitches, and the like. My two favorite replies to date: "My story according to me," and, from a woman who identified herself as a "reformed headhunter," "A piece of paper."

Experience teaches most managers that the résumé a job candidate presents as evidence of qualification is usually something less than gospel truth. Sometimes it contains embellishment, clever innuendo, distortions, wishful thinking, selective emphasis, overstatement, or outright deception. Despite the widely held wariness for the document—which is supposedly an accurate summary of experience and education—it remains a widely used tool for the first-pass screening of potential hires. Some high-tech résumés are scanned and electronically sorted, and electronic versions can be directly submitted via Internet mail.

When considering a candidate for possible employment, two things to keep in mind about that piece of paper (or collection of bits in the data bank):
1. assume that nothing may be as exactly stated and verify everything, and
2. remember that what is most important about the candidate—who they are—can never be represented by even the most credible and truthful résumé.

As a young man, I had the incomparable thrill of watching both my sons being born. Both boys came into the world with a clearly distinct *disposition*—visible at the very moment they were born. We may all be created equal, but surely we are all different. Scientists from a variety of disciplines continue, with dedication and energy, to research the age-old question of whether our complex and unique personalities are the result of nature (our family genes) or nurture (the environment and interactions each of us is brought up in).

The question of where a prospective employee's personality originated is irrelevant, but his or her personality is very relevant. People bring themselves to the job, not just their skills (and those skills may be an extension of their personality. At United Airlines, they talk—only half-jokingly—about the "customer service" gene). We don't hire qualifications or experience; we hire a whole person, with needs, wants, fears, dreams, doubts, desires, and hang-ups. We are likely to spend more waking hours with people we hire than with members of our family or friends.

> Only 20% of hiring failures are due to technical incompetence. The remainder are due to an individual's personality or emotional makeup.
> –Alan D. Davidson
> Psychologist, Hiring Expert

Having a good idea of the real person beneath the nice interview suit is critical because once you hire that person, you are going to be living with all of his or her quirks, and there's precious little you can do about those. People may react, adapt, adjust, conform or pretend, but they rarely change. Managers can easily waste too much of their time and mental energy playing tug-of-war with employees whose inclinations run contrary to the demands of their jobs or the cultural expectations of their employer. Likewise, employees waste precious energy and endure inevitably mounting stress in well-intended but doomed efforts to try to fit in or secretly fighting the system.

> It is certainly desirable to teach people how to do their jobs well, but unless their inner picture is one of competence, it doesn't matter how good your teaching is, you won't get competence—unless, of course, you're willing to stand over them all the time. You'll have to stand over them because the minute you don't, they'll revert to their dominant mental picture.
> –Lou Tice
> Executive Excellence

PERSONAL CONSIDERATIONS

Consider for a moment very personal factors that might significantly impact an indi-

vidual's job performance. These could include things such as one's attitude toward:
- the company's mission and priorities,
- satisfying customers,
- working with others,
- the particular management style of the boss,
- assigned pay and benefits,
- personal accountability for quality,
- supervisory oversight,
- performance incentives,
- physical working conditions,
- supporting multiple priorities,
- deadline pressures,
- attention to detail,
- continuous learning,
- applying acquired knowledge,
- following workplace rules,
- achieving assigned goals,
- working alone or as part of a group,
- cooperating with colleagues,
- following directives,
- initiating,
- change and ambiguity,
- and countless other factors in the workplace.

Which of the preceding attributes might be important criteria for assessing a job applicant? Even if these were listed on a résumé, could you rely on that information to assess how the candidate would really perform on the job?

A person's true performance in a job is driven by a host of uniquely personal factors that managers can't control, and barely even influence. People are motivated to work in their own way for their own reasons, including their personal values and their secret fears (real or imagined).

The better aligned an individual's personal motivations are with the requirements of his or her job and the tone, pace, and values of the workplace, the more naturally productive that person will be. For example, a person with a high need for structure performs better in a structured environment, while someone preferring a more freewheeling environment naturally produces better in a less structured workplace. While that's obvious when you read it, few managers select with such criteria in mind. There are a couple of reasons for that.

First, many managers have not really thought about the important, invisible aspects of their organization's culture, and they have little or no sense of the behavioral and personality requirements of an open position. Second, even if they did, they wouldn't know how to assess an applicant to see if there was a fit or not.

In the appendix at the end of this book (starting on page 208) you will find a schema of corporate culture.

Over thirty attributes of an organization's culture are described, and there are four descriptors (arranged on a continuum) to help you typify your company. The better you consciously and objectively understand your *company's* personality, the better you can assess a candidate's fit with it. The next chapter helps you analyze the work, and then the job, for which you are trying to hire someone.

> Our studies, two of which have been published in the Harvard Business Review, have proven that performance improves when there is a suitable "job match" between an individual's personality strengths and the requirements of a job.
> –User's Guide
> Caliper Corporation

Jobs are more than collections of tasks. They involve decisions, interactions with others, pacing, and physical demands, all of which can vary greatly from one job to another. Properly analyzing a job matters greatly to properly selecting the right person to fill it. After you complete this analysis, you will likely understand the job and the work better than you do now, and you may be surprised by how much you didn't know before.

How Social?

An example of a personality characteristic is the need to be with people. The presence of this characteristic, like all personality factors, is not a yes or no matter but rather a question of degree. For instance, I function competently in group interactions but do not enjoy them so much that I actively seek them.

My wife, on the other hand, likes being with people so much that she wants to go Christmas shopping in New York City when teeming crowds of locals and tourists from around the world jam-pack stores. Entering the middle of that crushing frenzy has the same appeal for me as catching a head cold. As a teacher surrounded by people all day long, Susan has a job that fits with her social needs. As a consultant and conference speaker, I have just about the perfect fit of solitude and interaction. Teaching and speaking have much in common, but are subtly different upon closer examination.

Another example: What separates inside customer service representatives from their outside sales counterparts? Both jobs require the capacity to listen and respond to customer needs and to present accurate information in a pleasing and effective way. Individuals in both positions must have the necessary ego strength to continue working productively even when customers complain and resist their efforts to serve them. But in each position, different personality requirements likely make a person much more suitable for one than the other.

One example of different work capabilities is the need for—or aversion to—an externally imposed work structure. The effective customer service rep likely enjoys responding to interactions initiated by the customer.

Effective sales representatives, on the other hand, must have the capacity to set priorities, plan their time, and generate customer interaction. The customer service rep must be comfortable in, or at least willing to withstand being in, one work environment of perhaps less than 100 square feet day after day.

By contrast, outside sales representatives cannot, for long periods of time, withstand the predictable sameness of constant workspace; they need to be out meeting customers in diverse and possibly widely scattered environments. Someone well-suited to the life of an outside sales person might well feel like a caged animal if required to become "chained to a desk." Likewise, the service person thrust out of his or her workplace's familiar confines might well feel lost and adrift.

When considering job characteristics and a candidate's personality factors, the more one understands about the true nature of each, the greater the probability of a good match.

The next chapter discusses how to profile all aspects of a job in order to identify the skills, competencies, and personal characteristics the person holding the job needs to fulfill the position's responsibilities. It lists more than a couple of dozen aspects of human performance that can be applied in an occupational setting.

Note: As there is no precedence for such a list as I've compiled it, there are no standard terms for describing the breadth of human capacity. Most of the literature on jobs divides the world into occupational behaviors, cognitive processes, or task functions. Such distinct groupings are no doubt useful to the specialized social scientists who study them. But these divisions seem artificial from the standpoint of a manager—someone who isn't researching a distinct part of the process but rather trying to comprehend and take responsibility for the whole of it. So, I created a simple naming scheme, explained in a bit more detail in the next chapter.

And two caveats: English has only so many words for concepts such as domain, and neither "dominion" nor "realm" seemed very appealing. I am not using the word in the sense that it appears in psychological literature, where it refers to a particular area of human thought. My connotation should be clear, but lest anyone become confused thinking about the other "domain," I wanted to be direct about it. Also, as must already be apparent, I use the word "personality" not in the clinical sense but in the broader lay sense of encompassing the totality of personhood: attitudes, behaviors, multiple mental processes—all the elements that make an individual an individual.

Most work requires people to draw on many aspects of themselves. Virtually all people have a part of their personality that they feel most comfortable with, and would emphasize in their work if given the choice.

Some people love to work with things and spend their time—on or off the job or both—handling things. A person whose dominant personal capacity is mechanical may work as a welder by day and tinker with old cars at night.

Someone else might prefer the conceptual capacity, drafting press releases for a living and then writing short stories to relax.

A socially dominated person may sell advertising time for a radio station as an occupation, and during off-hours volunteer for a high personal contact activity such as team coaching or fundraising.

A detail-oriented person whose profession is accounting might collect stamps or catalog recordings into a cross-referenced database for fun.

Someone dominant in the sensory capacity might be employed as a chef—an occupation requiring tactile, taste, smell, and visual skills—and unwind from the job's hectic pace by listening to music.

Not everyone is dominated by one sole capacity. Most people will find their interests and time spent on activities spanning two or more capabilities. The executive who earns her living preoccupied with conceptual and social capabilities may unwind by gardening and biking—leisure activities in the physical category.

Many occupations require acumen in several behavioral

dimensions of many capabilities. A food server at a busy restaurant must call on skills from the social, managerial, and time capabilities.

The strength of a capacity (the degree to which it has become a competency) for any one person might be assessed by how strongly that person feels a need for it, and how frequently or for how long a duration he or she dwells in it.

For example, a public relations account executive, responsible for the business relationship with the client and for supervising work the agency does on the client's behalf, must spend most of her time in the conceptual and social arenas. But for the PR agency to stay in business, the PR executive must file time reports and submit bills to the client. Thus, a competent PR executive must have the capacity to operate in the detail-oriented managerial capacity even though she may not enjoy it and is therefore not motivated by it in the least.

People who spend their days working in the capabilities in which they are quite comfortable derive more job satisfaction and suffer less stress than those who must toil at work outside their personally preferred performance domains.

The goal of natural selection hiring is to pair a person with work activities that mirror his or her preferred personal performance capacities. You wouldn't hire a fish to herd sheep, no matter how sincerely it pledged to work hard, learn the ropes, and "be the best employee you've ever had." And you wouldn't hire a cat as a swimming instructor, regardless of how many training programs in lifeguarding it had attended.

Capability vs. Suitability

There is a vast chasm between a person who is capable of mustering the necessary skills to complete a work task and someone who performs those tasks with aplomb, even joy. This is the difference between capability and suitability.

A person who can, with sufficient effort, exhibit behaviors from a given capacity is different from one who prefers to operate in that capacity.

For example, in my own work experience I functioned capably as a corporate executive. I had the requisite skills in my personal repertoire. But, upon reflection, I know that I lacked the appropriate intensity in the political and managerial capacities for much of that executive work to feel comfortable and natural. My own preferences, I now can see, were more conceptual, and less driven by a need for organizational behaviors—in fact, I feel an aversion to those political constraints. Giving in to the need to perform the required behaviors was something I could bear, but, over time, decreasingly so. Those behaviors began to feel like unnatural acts.

After leaving the corporate environment to seek a living as an independent consultant and to dwell in the conceptual and influential capacities without the constraints I felt in the political capacity, I frequently told friends and colleagues that I felt I had added at least ten years to my life. I probably have.

In conclusion: Because one can doesn't necessarily mean one should.

Effectiveness in even many entry-level jobs may require competence in several capacities, even some that are not obvious. For example, consider the commonplace entry-level job of retail clerk in a clothing store. It requires behaviors from several capacities, including interpersonal, numerical, influential, spatial, and analytical.

The more varied the tasks of a job, the more likely a greater number of capacities will be involved, and the less likely someone will be uniformly competent. Is this an argument for narrow job responsibilities? Not at all. Job enrichment may well spring from offering people a chance to indulge in the many capacities and potential competencies they bring with them when they join a payroll. It also points to the need for both careful screening of an applicant's inclinations as well as training and development opportunities.

As more organizations move toward "cross-training" and self-managing work teams—broad application of multi-capacity competence—staffing with people who have competencies in complementary capacities will become increasingly important.

Fit for Duty

The basic issue in finding a well-suited person to fill a particular job opening comes down to *fit*. The fundamental question to be asked and answered is this: How will a given job applicant fit with this job, in this organization, working for this supervisor, with these coworkers, in this particular environment, at this time?

A person works tirelessly and joyfully for unreasonable hours. Do they do it because they are chasing bonuses or running from the boss's wrath and whip? Could it be for other reasons?

> Work can and should give you a sense of joy. You spend 60 percent of your life doing work or getting ready for it. So to dismiss your work by saying 'I'm just doing this to pay the bills' seems like an enormous trade-off.
> –Richard Leider
> Author, Counselor

Think of the perpetually self-propelled computer programmer toiling away into the wee night hours fueled only by a passion for programming and maybe a few candy bars washed down with soda or coffee. It's a stereotype rooted in archetypal truth. Such tireless dedication to professional duties is also often true for a lawyer, administrative assistant, sales rep, police officer, caterer, researcher, doctor, teacher, retailer, manager, truck driver, woodworker, musician, mason, or journalist. People truly suited to their work do it at once slavishly and joyfully without a remnant of resentment, without need for either prodding or motivation. They work at their work for its intrinsic fulfillment. It is nothing less than *self-enrichment*—in the potent psychic sense more than the feeble fiscal one.

For people who are motivated by it, work is *art*; work serves as expression, an extension of the self. The successful lobbyist, coach, teacher, salesperson or litigator enjoys influencing others. The successful accountant, quality specialist, regulator or janitor delights in order and control. The entrepreneur, photographer, designer or decorator delights in creating. The counselor, veterinarian, minister or nurse is sustained by nurturing. People in harmony with their work are energized by it. People in the wrong line of work, or working in an unsatisfactory environment, become drained or perhaps even killed by it.

There's a rhythm, a song each of us wishes to play in life. For the lucky few who find well-suited occupations, work is the instrument.

Checks and Balance

Every job comes with both fiscal and psychic paychecks. The less satisfying the job, the fewer the psychic paychecks and the more likely the employee will demand additional money. There's a mental scorecard in people's heads. It has two columns: monetary rewards and emotional rewards. When the two columns are basically even (and the money column records a fair, competitive wage), people do their jobs at an acceptable level. When the money column is still at an acceptable level and the emotional column records additional entries, productivity goes up. When the emotional column shows few positive entries, or records negative ones, the demand for more money goes up.

Many bosses believe employees are motivated by money. Most employees say non-fiscal factors influence their work motivation and productivity more. The most important emotional factor to people is to enjoy their work. Given the amount of time spent working—at the expense of anything else—this shouldn't be surprising. What contributes to people enjoying their work? Well, certainly a great many things, but at the top of the list of most important drivers of satisfaction is feeling at home with work, feeling that comfortable fit. Working hard and working well come easily and naturally to people who operate in synch with, or in harmony with, their tasks.

While speaking at management conferences, I meet literally thousands of businesspeople in the course of a year. I have never met one who complained he or she was overpaid. In fact, I can recall only very rare complaints about being underpaid. But there is no shortage of frustrations, disappointments, and hurts. And these are the bosses! At all levels in an organization, it is the emotional ledger that runs the deficit, and the one that people pay serious attention to every day.

Carefully match people to their work so that their emotional scorecard fills up simply by showing up and getting to work.

Feels Like Home

While a job candidate should have a natural affinity for the work in the open position, a match between personality and the corporate culture is just as important. "You can take an outstanding scientist, put them in an uncomfortable organizational environment and they'll fail miserably," observes employment expert Lee Bowes.

> We do not own you; we do, however, rent your behavior for a good portion of every week.
>
> –Joseph Semrod
> Chairman, Summit Bancorporation

It's no wonder. Every firm casts its unique shadow over even standard jobs. Some firms expect their employees to toil—or at least be at the work site—long days and nights and weekends, as if, somehow, that signified deep commitment to the cause. Other companies consider people who work with anything but a somewhat detached, laissez-faire work attitude to be suffering some kind of serious imbalance.

Still other outfits cultivate an aggressive, internally competitive environment where survival of the fittest applies not only in the market but also within the employing organization itself. Some organizations operate almost as a cult, with a strong allegiance to a publicly charismatic leader; some expect all employees to exhibit a deep sense of belonging to the group during work hours at the workplace and after hours outside the place of business. Some organizations direct in fine detail every move an employee makes on the job; others expect employees to be responsible for methods as well as outcomes, while still others have no such overarching expectations and customs vary from work group to work group.

> If you don't fit into the culture, you'll be rejected like a bad organ transplant.
> –Kate Wendleton
> President, Five O'Clock Club

> For any number of jobs, the most important requisite for doing well is fitting in.
> –Lee Bowes
> author, CEO, America Works

Somewhere, someone is well-suited to each of these diverse environments. No one is suited to all of them. Woe to those miserable folks who thought themselves fortunate to be hired into a line of work that they loved, only to find it was at the wrong company. They're destined to strike sour notes as the right instrument in the wrong band playing in the wrong key.

Dangerous Impressions

Many managers believe they can assess a job candidate's uniquely personal factors and his or her probable fit to the job and culture during an interview by getting a gut feel for the applicant, or assessing the chemistry they sense in the brief interaction. That's just as self-defeating as pretending that personality issues don't matter on the job.

Take note of this: Verbally skilled (or well-prepared

and rehearsed) job interviewees fool many hiring managers. And unfortunately, less verbally adept candidates can, just as easily, inadvertently mislead a manager who relies on superficial impressions. Imagine hiring a housekeeper who interviews like Felix Unger but turns out to be Oscar Madison. Or turning away the most gifted, most meticulous housekeeper because you didn't immediately sense a great rapport at the interview's outset.

The stakes can be much higher. If you were hiring a kindergarten teacher, customer service agent, police officer, airline pilot, or surgeon, wouldn't you want a more accurate and reliable read on the applicant's emotional stability than your casual impressions can give you?

We explore personality and behavioral preference assessments in Chapter 7, and take up the topic of effectively interviewing in much greater depth in Chapter 8. The point here is to acknowledge the need to intentionally and methodically assess for personality factors when searching for people whose true selves naturally fit both their prospective work and your organization.

Once an applicant fills a job opening, you manage the person, not the position. It's important to know who the person is before the worker starts.

Part Two
The Natural Selection Hiring Method™

Chapter Four
Define the Job to Define Who You Hire

Chapter Five
Predicting the Future by Sitting in Judgment

Chapter Six
Assessing Applicants: A Process

Chapter Seven
This Is a Test... This Is *Only* a Test

Chapter Eight
Interviewing: "So, Tell Me About Myself"

Chapter Four

Define the Job to Define Who You Hire

> Many companies don't know what they want. When there is a vacancy all they try to do is replace old Charlie or Suzie. They don't look at how the job has changed.
>
> —Jay Jarrell
> Human Resources Consultant
> in the Pittsburgh Business Times

How do you know what kind of person you need to fill an open position with your firm? Before you start recruiting, interviewing, assessing, or hiring, you need to specify the ideal candidate, but probably in a way you never have before.

Obviously, you intend to hire a person capable of "doing the job." But what is that? The job is, to be sure, a set of tasks. But it's much more than that. Chances are the current job description for the open position, even if it's new, doesn't begin to get at what's truly important about the job, so it's likely of limited value for guiding you through your candidate assessment and selection decisions.

Some hard-charging managers proclaim, "I know what I

want!" in defining the ideal hire. Yet with the rarest of exceptions, most managers have, at best, only identified the technical skills necessary for executing the job's tasks (for example, produce financial reports using computers). The glaring omission in specifying the ideal jobholder's profile is having defined neither systematically nor thoroughly the personal qualities required to accomplish the job's desired outcomes. Here are some examples of what I mean:

- broad understanding of central business objectives and key business measures,
- confidence to work with and make suggestions to the senior managers who are the customers of the reports produced by this position,
- analytic skills to discern variables that potentially should be tracked and the metrics by which to measure them,
- attention to detail and commitment to quality to produce accurate reports,
- visual competency to produce reports that provide maximum information at a glance,
- capacity to work productively in a pressured deadline environment,
- patience and willingness to change output in response to changing conditions and the whims of internal customers,
- a team orientation to influence and work cooperatively with colleagues in various financial departments and the information systems group without formal authority to direct their efforts.

Hiring managers, therefore, typically have neglected to specify vitally important capacities needed in the person on whom they'll ultimately depend to do what needs to be done. Not surprisingly, hiring managers often get what they said they wanted but not what they truly needed. (Worse, many times they hire someone they thought was just like what they wanted, but—because of imprecision in the screening and interviewing process—the person wasn't even that! It's very easy to mishire people for jobs at which, realistically, their innate shortcomings will prevent them from ever performing beyond a mediocre level—even with managerial interventions, training, incentives and other forms of attempted human retrofitting. The critical issue of assessing job applicants is taken up in Chapters 5, 6, 7, and 8.)

THE NATURE OF A JOB

Before defining the process by which you can better define a job to better define the ideal candidate for it, let's take a moment to reconsider this familiar but changing concept of a job. A manager hires someone to fill a job (position or post) in order to do work. Of course, in its classic sense, work is a collection of actions, duties, and tasks. But in our technologically advanced society, work that is performed by people rather than machines usually necessitates human qualities (or a machine would already be doing the tasks). It is in terms of human qualities that jobs need to be defined, and often they are not.

Fast Forward to the Past

The way most of us think about jobs is largely the product of the Industrial Revolution of the nineteenth century. That social revolution combined emerging technology with a new way of organizing people's labor to enable large-scale production in factories and on farms. The mass production concept changed the very notion of work for most people. Before the Industrial Revolution, most people who weren't farmers earned their livelihoods as self-employed merchants, self-reliant craftsmen, or all-purpose hands for hire. Working in this manner usually afforded people a holistic view of their efforts' processes, tasks, and outcomes.

Take for example the work of fashioning furniture. The woodworker of 150 years ago making a stool may well have dealt single-handedly (well, he probably used both hands) with the whole production, from designing the piece to acquiring materials, fashioning the raw materials, assembling the piece, finishing it, and selling it to a buyer. By contrast, people laboring in a post-industrial work scheme based on the division of labor have their efforts parsed into discrete, specialized, and repetitive tasks. Someone might only turn a lathe to produce one leg of a stool, exclusively and repetitively, before passing this fragmented piece along the production process to someone else who is also responsible for only a small chunk of the whole. The specialized worker thus is extremely proficient at a small number of tasks, a system that speeds up the rate of production and lowers costs (as well as job satisfaction for a great many people, unfortunately).

Today, the legacy of the Industrial Revolution is thriving. Many jobs clearly descend from the division of labor school of work design. At the same time, the pendulum is swinging back from the mechanized, isolated parts model of work to one in which workers have a greater orientation to the whole of their work. In manufacturing, the separate, individual posts on assembly lines are giving way to collaborative, self-managing work groups that plan their own schedules, buy their own materials, monitor their own quality, rotate jobs, and share collective rewards for performance.

In both manufacturing and service-based organizations, functional departments increasingly exist in a process-oriented environment where work is both planned and executed through cross-functional and self-governing teams (which may include members from marketing, finance, engineering, production, and so on). In this newer work structure, workers with specialized functional expertise have more responsibility for understanding the company's broad business objectives and the processes behind achieving them. No longer working in the relative seclusion of executing isolated tasks, employees now do their work by interacting with colleagues. This necessitates that they possess high levels of interpersonal skills as well as technical knowledge.

So, what does this have to do with better describing a job in order to hire better? Everything. To think of a job as a mere collection of tasks may miss the larger and more important piece of the success equation—the human components that influence how those tasks are completed and therefore how well they are completed. In today's competitive, time-sensitive, and service-demanding market, those human factors may make all the difference in the world.

Before you hire a person—a unique bundle of capabilities, experiences, needs, and shortcomings—you really need to understand what you're hiring that person to do, and, in turn, what kind of person it takes to do that work. In defining a job, there are two basic components to describe:

1. What characterizes the job's important tasks? (For example, does it require heavy lifting, or constructing mathematical computations, or typing, or writing in a particular language?)
2. What are the personal attributes that are required to perform the job? (For example, knowledge of a particular body of information, or the ability to present proposals confidently to senior executives, or the capacity to innovate in response to changing market conditions, or the ability to consistently follow very strict guidelines without deviation, and so on.)

DOES ANYBODY REALLY KNOW WHAT JOB IT IS?

How can you expect to accurately answer the two questions above? How does anyone know what a given job really is? A supervisor has an idea of the work done in the jobs reporting to him or her. But another supervisor in the same department may have a different idea of it. The same holds true for two incumbents actually doing the job—they may not do the job exactly alike, and there is an especially great deal of potential difference between the approaches of an old salt and a greenhorn. The ideas of the people actually holding the job may vary considerably from their supervisors', which, in turn, might vary widely from those of professional job analysts working in the organization's human resource department.

How can there be so many different ideas about the same job? For many reasons. Casually describing work responsibilities gives rise to many potential distortions. One person may focus on some infrequent tasks that seem more important or impressive than the job's true thrust. Another person may make a parallel error—focusing on frequently repeated tasks that are, in themselves, relatively minor in impact (for example, an executive may check for e-mail messages many times a day, but that is hardly the thrust of his or her post). Some people may simply overlook tasks or over- or under-estimate either the frequency or importance of certain tasks to performing the job.

To eliminate the potential confusion, ambiguities, and contradictions that can arise from informal or anecdotal conceptions of a job, a more disciplined approach to looking at a specific job (a body of work to be completed to achieve a specific purpose) is required.

Some academics and consultants who have considered this issue have constructed formal instruments for "job analysis" such as the Job Element Inventory and the Position Analysis Questionnaire (PAQ). The PAQ, for example, analyzes a job by looking at work behaviors, job characteristics, and working conditions in 195 questions grouped into six sections. The PAQ is designed to be used by someone with at least a college education, and is often deployed by human resources specialists for collecting quantitative data about a wide variety of jobs such as those in a very large corporation or governmental organization.

In contrast to academically oriented instruments, the methods suggested below are for use by a manager without specialized human resources training who wishes to better understand the work for which she or he is responsible. In profiling a job using the Natural Selection Hiring Method, the focus is on specifying what a person doing the job actually does to achieve the desired outcomes and the manner in which those tasks are performed. The insights gained from this profiling process should be applicable both for hiring appropriate personnel and then developing their skills and competence during their tenure.

Note: The profiling of a job as suggested here—the analysis of a position's work content and of the characteristics needed in someone in order to produce that work—is different from what is commonly known as job evaluation. Job evaluation focuses on assessing the economic value of a job or occupation. Job evaluation studies attempt to establish the worth of a position in order to compare jobs or occupations for setting pay rates, resolving questions of "comparable pay for comparable work" and the like. A job evaluation attempts to assess a position's potential impact on the organization or external environment, its work complexities, education or specialized training requirements, latitude for decision-making, level of responsibility, the nature of the job holder's interactions with others within and outside of the organization, independence from supervision, and so on. Such considerations are distinct from and beyond the intent of the Natural Selection Hiring Method, which focuses on matching an individual's capacities to work requirements.

Work According to the Government

Since 1938, the U.S. federal government has been codifying jobs by workers' titles and tasks to support public employment programs that help to place job seekers. The Labor Department's Dictionary of Occupational Titles (DOT) lists brief descriptions of duties for some 12,741 occupations under an even greater abundance of titles in 1,404 pages. It includes information about what workers in a given job do, the tasks they perform, the machines or tools they operate, the kind of instructions they typically follow and the judgments they typically make, the working environment of the job, as well as ratings for the job's physical demands, and the required general educational level and specific vocational preparation necessary to perform the job. This information, along with other data, can be used by a company to compare a given job to others for setting salaries, career planning, identifying training needs, and so on.

The DOT lists job titles from abalone diver through zoo veterinarian. It chronicles the diversity of our multifaceted economy with its huge array of entries. These include such intriguing posts as jawbone breaker (listed for the meat products industry—there is no industry classification for organized crime), muck boss (found in many industries, but the title is to be found on a business card only in the mine and quarry industry), jacket changer (a post in a foundry, not a suit shop), nickel cleaner (found, apparently, anywhere dirty nickels need a shine), feather-crushing-machine operator (a fowl occupation for sure), and nipper (which the Feds say applies to any industry). Then there's nitroglycerin supervisor and raw-cheese worker (two workers one hopes would never bump into each other).

Codifying the diverse, ever-changing richness of the free enterprise system as expressed in tens of millions of jobs and then capturing it all between the covers of a printed book is, of course, a largely futile effort. The DOT, the long-time standard for job classification, is, as the government openly admits, woefully outdated (there is no entry for Web master, and there are no headings for Internet-related posts), having been updated most recently in 1991. Since then, Labor Department officials have focused on creating a computerized database of work undertaken throughout the U.S. economy. The government has dubbed the computer-based project O*NET, for Occupational Information Network. O*NET will be a comprehensive database system for collecting, organizing, describing and disseminating data on job characteristics along with the attributes of workers who typically fill a given job.

O*NET, according to the official proclamation from the U.S. Department of Labor's Employment and Training Administration, "provides a new conceptual framework that reflects the advanced technologies, adaptable workplace structures and wide-ranging skills required by today's changing workplace." The system's first functional release is targeted for sometime in 2000. But your task of assessing the characteristics of jobs in your organization should not depend on a newfangled monster database from Uncle Sam. No matter how slick and spiffy it is, it is not going to tell you what you need to know to make a good hiring selection for the work that needs to be done in your company.

Every company defines its work structures and the responsibilities of a given post differently in keeping with its unique needs, structure, and culture. You must fully define the jobs found in your organization by seeing them exactly as they are, not by lumping them together with similar-sounding generic titles and characteristics-in-common from an amalgamated database created by synthesizing bureaucratic data collections. It is the differences from the generic that help define what is unique about your organization and what is important to your selection process. Only by fully describing the work and its organization into a unique job as it exists exclusively within your company can you fully describe the unique person best suited to filling it productively.

PROFILING A GIVEN JOB

The process for creating a job profile is outlined in Figure 4-1 on page 67 and explained in greater detail below.

Here is an overview of a simple process you can use for cre-

> Selection operates at the boundaries of the organization. It necessarily exposes decision-makers to the environment they operate in, provides access to information about the world in which the organization operates, and forces choices about its relationship with that environment. The process of defining standards for positions also reflects and reinscribes the organization's priorities and direction. Emphasizing one set of skills over another in the selection process communicates to employees and students how the organization defines good work. Thus, the selection process is one that provides the opportunity and challenge of continually redefining standards in relation to the stakeholders of the organization, both inside and outside.
>
> –Susan Sturm and Lani Guinier
> Professors of Law
> University of Pennsylvania,
> California Law Review, July 1996

ating a detailed picture of a job, so you can create a detailed profile of a suitable candidate. A more detailed approach, with a fill-in-the-blanks matrix, appears at the end of this chapter. (*Note:* The diagram in Figure 4-1 indicates the analytic flow for a single outcome produced by a lone task. In fact, a job may have several outcomes, each produced by multiple tasks. When analyzing a job, complete the flow for all outcomes, all tasks, and all related personal capacities and work behaviors.)

1. Define the outcomes of the position. Why does the job exist? What impact, results, or benefit is the position expected to deliver? Specify the ultimate results the position creates.

Example. *Position:* administrative assistant. Outcome of work: increases effectiveness and productivity of [a particular executive or members of an assigned work group], leveraging their time for higher productivity and value.

Notice how there was not one word about taking messages, scheduling meetings, ordering lunch, or even working as a member of a team. The focus here is on the net result. If you can't define this, you either don't need or don't understand the position. If you don't understand it, you can't manage it to its greatest contribution. And you certainly can't hire a person ideally suited for it.

2. List major job functions. *Complete this sentence:* "The per-

Define the Job to Define Who You Hire 67

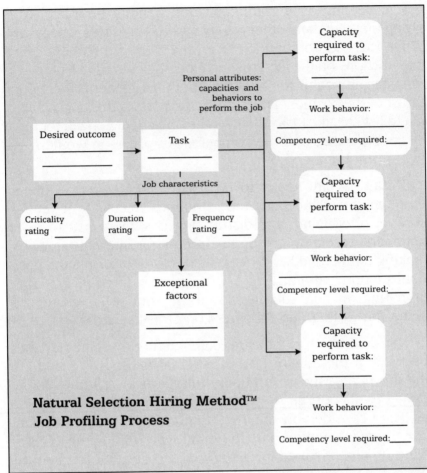

Figure 4-1. Profiling a job—in order to hire the best person to fill it—means analyzing work by defining its ideal outcomes, and then breaking the work into the tasks required to produce the outcomes, and then identifying the kind of personal attributes ("capacities") that the jobholder needs in order to produce the tasks—and results—successfully. A given body of work may have several identifiable outcomes. A given outcome may require numerous tasks performed by someone with multiple capacities (defined in greater detail later in this chapter).

son in this position will accomplish its objectives by..." In our example of the administrative assistant, these job functions might include handling administrative tasks for the work group, serving as a communication conduit between work group members and other organization employees, and so on. While there is no specific place for entering the overarching job functions on the Job Profiling Process depicted in Figure 4-1, this step is useful for thinking about the general functional thrust of the position. From this broad perspective, you can begin to list specific tasks that can then be characterized for their distinct qualities and the competencies a person would need to perform them.

3. Detail specific tasks to be performed. In our example, these might include answering phones; receiving, opening, sorting, prioritizing, and distributing incoming mail to team members; reserving conference rooms for internal meetings; making airline and hotel reservations for the people the position supports; drafting replies to routine internal inquiries; preparing, in publication-ready form, routine status reports about the work group's progress on projects; and so on.

4. List distinctive or unusual components or characteristics of tasks. If the administrative assistant will need to perform the job duties aboard a floating platform in Alaska's Bering Straits to support an oil exploration team, that colors the job as being considerably different than a functionally equivalent one based in an office park in Hometown, USA. In the Job Profiling Process pictured in Figure 4-1, the unusual characteristics of the job tasks would be listed under the "exceptional factors" box. The type of considerations that would be useful to note include characterizations of the job tasks such as:

- dangerous conditions or unusual risk (as in police, firefighting, or rescue work);
- severe deadline pressure (as in broadcast news);
- contentious or combative communications situations (as in a complaint or media relations department);
- extensive travel or unusual hours or working conditions (for example, auditing livestock herds by physically counting them in the field);
- complex, uncommon, or imprecise reporting relationships

(such as reporting to several bosses, some in distant locales, or having "dotted line" or matrix supervisory reporting, and so on) or working remotely—either in a geographically remote area or simply removed from supervision or other organization contacts.

5. **Define the relative importance of each task.** Of all the job's tasks, which are absolutely central to achieving the position's objectives? In other words, which tasks must be done well for the job to achieve its aims, and which tasks could be done at a less-than-proficient level or not done at all? Naturally, you would like all the tasks in a job done and done well. But the reality is that no candidate you're likely to hire will perfectly embody all the necessary capabilities in exactly the right measure to completely fill a job's performance requirements. To strike the right balance between getting the job done perfectly and actually finding someone to do it, you must honestly assess the relative importance of each task to achieving the job's mission. You do this through three valuations:

- how vital a task is to achieving the job's outcome (called *criticality*),
- how often a task is performed (called *frequency*), and
- for what length of time a task is performed (called *duration*).

Scale for Criticality
- Absolutely critical (the job objectives cannot be accomplished without this)
- Necessary but not critical
- Part of job, relatively minor importance

Scale for Frequency
- Constantly
- Many times daily
- At least once daily
- A few times a week
- Weekly
- Monthly
- Infrequently

Scale for Duration
- Continuously
- Several hours daily
- An hour or more
- Several minutes
- A minute or Less

The frequency and duration ratings can give an indication of a task's relative intensity in a job, which can help determine how adept or suitable the potential new hire needs to be in performing the task. A quick example: Someone with a low tolerance for detail work probably could do an adequate job filling out a weekly report that took less than an hour to prepare. But that same person might grow frustrated and produce inaccurate work if forced to spend several hours a day preparing such reports—an even graver concern if such reports were considered absolutely critical to the job's mission.

RATING THE HUMAN COMPONENTS

In addition to rating the relative importance of job tasks, you will also need to rate the human qualities that underlie the task performance in terms of how proficient someone holding the job needs to be at performing the task in order to produce acceptable results (this is called *competence*).

> Effective job/role design can help reduce personnel costs, streamline work processes, increase productivity and employee empowerment, enhance job satisfaction and provide greater scheduling for the employee.
> –Kenneth H. Pritchard, CCP in a white paper for the Society of Human Resource Management, 1997

Scale for Competence
A. Mastery
B. Advanced competence
C. Competent
D. Developmental

In a given job, the competence levels for various tasks within a job can be different from one another. A sales representative newly hired to call on senior executive customers may be expected to have advanced competence in securing appointments while only possessing a developmental skill level for operating the company's custom computer software program for sending internal e-mail. An internal candidate for the sales job who had mastery level e-mail skills but who lacked sufficient interpersonal or self-management capacities to perform the job would be unacceptable.

How Much Detail? How Important?

In profiling a job, is a great level of detail necessary? Only if you want to be accurate. Stepping back for a "big picture" assessment of a job makes it less likely that you'll accurately portray its true nature. Studies by workplace psychologists bear out that holistic job analysis is less accurate than "decomposed" or component analysis. Sweeping assessments simply assume too much and overlook too much. That said, a high level of detail also could be self-defeating. Detailing and analyzing every minor, infrequent task that might fall within a year's work in a job can be a waste of your time and probably won't matter a whit when hiring. Strike a balance by identifying truly critical tasks; to do that, you need to spend some time observing and inquiring about a job's true nature.

The potential for error in a job analysis profile can be quite costly. Overestimate the qualifications you need in a new hire and you'll probably pay more than you need by attracting skills you don't need. Plus, if you hire an overqualified person, he or she likely will get bored with it and suffer demotivation, reducing productivity and increasing the probability of departing the company for a more suitable challenge. That would leave you with a vacancy, zero productivity, and unnecessary recruiting, selection, and hiring costs. Likewise, underestimating a job's true nature by a broad-brush assessment means you likely will fill it with someone who lacks the capacity to do what truly needs to be done. Again, productivity will be low while the chance of turnover will be high. Your best bet is to invest the time to profile the job accurately so that you can accurately hire to the job's actual specifications.

If you need additional incentive to take the time to profile a post, recognize that there are incentives to be found in employment law. The Equal Employment Opportunity Commission standards require that a job analysis "should describe all important work behaviors, their relative importance and their level of frequency or difficulty." Why would the federal government stipulate job analysis requirements? To ensure compliance with equal opportunity laws and the requirements of the Americans with Disabilities Act.

If you deny employment to someone in a protected class (a member of a minority group or someone who may be a potential victim of age discrimination or of not making reasonable accommodation for a disability), you may be called upon to prove that this person was, in fact, not qualified. If you have nothing to adequately tie your standards of qualification to an actual ability to perform the job—in other words, a job profile showing the relationship between outcomes, tasks, and the required personal characteristics of the person doing the job—you're going to have a more difficult time defending your judgment of candidates.

With a job profile, you can show the business purpose for selecting people with certain characteristics while rejecting those without them. Without a job profile to justify your candidate requirements and assessments, they look arbitrary and are ripe for accusations of unfair discrimination.

Performance Domains and Capacities for Work

After analyzing the expected outcomes for a body of work and identifying the tasks necessary to produce them, you need to think beyond tasks and get to the personal level. Consider this question: What kind of personal attributes are necessary for success in this position?

Take, for example, the role of a person's temperament in job performance. A nurse doing intake processing in a big-city emergency room may require a different temperament (degree of patience, decisiveness, speed, and efficiency of verbal communication) than a nurse doing intake at a rural convalescent center for elderly patients. The list of duties in their respective job descriptions might be almost identical:
- welcome patient,
- obtain medical history,
- perform initial assessment of care needs, and so on.

Even the job candidate qualifications might be identical:
- nursing license,
- three or more years of clinical experience,
- strong verbal communication skills, and so on.

The requisite technical skill and work experience for these posts, when lined up side by side, might appear nearly identical. Still, there can be a world of difference between people who are technically prepared for a position by having the stipulated skill sets and those whose less visible attributes make them a bad, good, or fantastic match for the unique demands of the position.

So how do you typify the characteristics of a job so that you know what personal traits to seek in job applicants? Here is a taxonomy of human capabilities that people draw on or exhibit when they perform work. Grouped into four broad categories called *performance domains* (see Figure 4-2, page 74), they are further divided into *capacities* and *work behaviors*.

Defining Terms

This book introduces a taxonomy of work-related personal characteristics. Here is an explanation of the terms involved. A job is a collection of expected outcomes, and the work tasks that produce those outcomes, as well as the desired behaviors exhibited by someone performing those

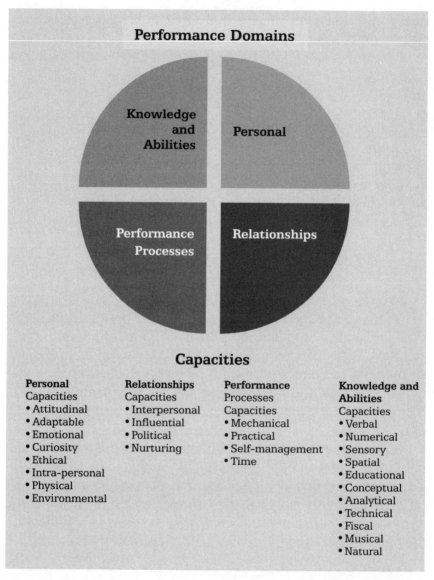

Figure 4-2. A person's capability to perform work functions can be described in four main performance domains and their related capacities. Within each capacity there are numerous work behaviors.

work tasks.

When an individual demonstrates a particular quality that is applicable to doing the work of a job, they possess a capacity, which can exist in varying degrees. Every person embodies a unique mix of capacities, and possesses any given capacity to a different degree than anyone else. The capacities are grouped into four performance domains—general areas in which people demonstrate competence to do a job.

Every job requires a unique set of capacities from the person filling it; some capacities are more critical to performing a job well than are others. What a person actually does on the job—his or her actions—is called work behavior. (When a particular work behavior has been developed to a high level of proficiency through training or experience, it becomes a skill that can be measured in degrees of competence.) The degree to which a job is performed well varies according to how critical the worker's capacities are to fully accomplishing the job's aims and the degree to which the worker embodies and demonstrates the necessary level of competence in work behaviors required to execute tasks.

Why people do what they do comes from personal values (their feelings about what is important to them). What an individual is likely capable of doing well is called potential.

Competence and mastery in performing a job depend on a person sufficiently embodying the various capacities in each of the performance domains that are necessary to achieving a job's objectives. An individual's competence to perform a job depends on his or her having the sufficient mixture of the relevant capacities (in other words, all the necessary qualities to the degree necessary to consistently produce the job's desired outcomes).

The four performance domains in the Natural Selection Hiring Method group characteristics differently than the traditional way industrial psychologists have categorized personal attributes related to work. The classic scheme is Knowledge, Skills, Abilities, and Other characteristics (KSAO). Knowledge and abilities constitute one of the four performance domains; its capacities include the classic verbal and numeric cognitive abilities along with many others, including specific technical knowledge that is applicable to a particular job.

Specifying behaviors and characteristics in the other performance domains—personal, relationships, and performance processes—underscores the importance of these capabilities, skills, and behaviors, which might otherwise be lost in the broadly generic KSAO label. These performance areas rate as vitally important in performing most every work. Given the importance of self-management, process management, and interpersonal relationships in today's service-, knowledge-, and team-based workplace, the classic KSAO grouping for worker characteristics strikes me as terribly inadequate. The four performance domains more explicitly communicate the four essential components of every job applicant's competence that truly matter in delivering job performance:

- attitude, resilience, and self-control;
- capability to relate to coworkers and customers;
- processes for self-managing work; and
- knowledge, imagination, and thinking capabilities.

The work behaviors listed within each capacity are far from exhaustive. Consider this broad menu of actions related to job performance as a starting point for defining the exact characteristics you require from a person to perform a job. You can further refine the list of general capabilities within categories by adding greater levels of detail.

For example, within the knowledge and abilities domain there is the verbal capacity. It includes the work behavior "Writes to a standard." If you were hiring a technical writer, you'd want to specify the standard of writing that makes the job distinct from, say, writing radio advertising copy. (In actually defining the ideal candidate for the technical writing job by completing the process and forms found later in this chapter, you would also specify other personal characteristics central to fulfilling job requirements. In doing this, you'd likely find some personal characteristics that would separate a technical writer from an advertising writer. These might include making distinctions between the analytic and conceptual capacities in the knowledge and abilities domain.)

The thrust of the Natural Selection Hiring Method is *behavioral*. A specific person's capability to do specific work comes down to whether he or she can behave in a way that's desirable and appropriate for the job. Recall the discussion from Chapter 3 about the difference between understanding something and being competent at it. In the list that follows, you'll note that the work capacities are expressed as verbs, words that describe action. That's because the person you hire is being hired to do something. Even when considering how someone performs work (his or her attitude, cooperativeness, and so on), you can point to behaviors that model the desired attributes.

For example, a "nice" receptionist can be defined by behaviors that create a welcoming environment for visitors and show a genuine interest in them. Those actions could include greeting visitors with a smile, using their names, asking if they'd like something to drink while waiting, checking with the party being visited to be sure he or she is aware the visitors have arrived, and so on.

The specific job tasks of announcing visitors, offering them refreshments, and the like are definable in a job description. The personal capacities to be welcoming by presenting a pleasant disposition, demonstrating genuine interest in the comfort of guests, and the like are not job tasks per se but rather the personal orientation of the individual performing the job.

Anyone who has ever heard a surly receptionist (or sales clerk or waiter) gruffly snap, "May I help you?" knows the difference between someone only going through the prescribed motions and someone who actually wants to help. The most productive receptionist is likely to be someone who is already inclined toward these thoughtful social gestures because he or she exhibits relevant behaviors from the relationships domain in the interpersonal and nurturing capacities.

Pick any job and you probably can find a parallel set of examples that demonstrate the important distinction between someone who simply executes a job description's prescribed tasks—emptily going through the motions—and someone who embodies the personal characteristics that fuel those tasks with commitment and joy, and is thereby propelled to higher levels of quality and productivity.

In clarifying a job, your task, aided by the tools in this chapter, is to complete this sentence:

> In order to be successful at this job, a person must produce results that include _____, by performing tasks that include _____, by behaving in a manner described as _____, and under conditions that include _____ .

At this point, you may want to review the list of performance characteristics to familiarize yourself with them. Lest you think the variety of capacities is overwhelming, understand that when it comes time to select someone to fill an open job, you'll likely assess candidates for only a small percentage of all the capacities applicable to a job. But knowing the key characteristics that drive performance helps you better understand the factors most likely to make a person successful in a certain job.

1. Domain: *Personal*

Attitudinal: Expressing disposition, commitment, and feelings.
- Enjoys work, takes pride and personal satisfaction from it
- Projects positiveness
- Presents self with pleasant demeanor
- Gives freely
- Takes appropriately
- Defers to moral and organizational authority
- Respects others
- Engages in humor appropriately
- Displays passion appropriately
- Exudes determination
- Perseveres in the face of obstacles and setbacks

- Volunteers and contributes freely
- Persists
- Seeks and is comfortable with, risk
- Follows directives
- Serves with joy
- Laughs at self
- Complains with tact and focus on the mission
- Respects all others

Adaptable: Responding to changing conditions.
- Seeks or welcomes new experiences
- Assesses evolving situations
- Accepts uncertainty
- Operates effectively amid ambiguity
- Considers alternatives
- Adjusts, changes, and reinvents appropriately

Emotional: Showing and relating to personal feelings.
- Exhibits emotional stability
- Expresses feelings appropriately
- Intuits and understands others' feelings
- Maintains self-control and emotional equilibrium in uncertain, changing, unexpected, and emotionally charged environments
- Receives criticism good-naturedly
- Recovers quickly to a state of emotional equilibrium after suffering a setback or minor crisis

Curiosity: Questioning what is.
- Wonders why
- Challenges the status quo and convention
- Tests assumptions

Ethical: Behaving in accord with moral standards.
- Complies with legal and moral codes
- Exhibits integrity
- Deals honestly
- Seeks and accepts accountability
- Stands firm for the right course of action even when it is

difficult or unpopular
- Invests full professional energies into work responsibilities
- Behaves maturely, responsibly, and honorably at all times regarding all things
- Opposes, avoids, and corrects, to the extent possible, offenses, slights, and injustices

Intra-personal: Relating to one's self.
- Thinks for self
- Respects self
- Understands own needs and motivations
- Knows strengths and deficiencies
- Recognizes own beliefs, biases, and prejudices
- Trusts own instincts and judgments
- Acts with confidence
- Functions with self-reliance
- Behaves courageously
- Displays self-discipline

Physical: Using one's body.
- Embodies strength
- Moves within necessary range of movement
- Displays dexterity and agility
- Exhibits coordination
- Displays stamina
- Appears presentably

Environmental: Functioning within particular conditions.
- Works productively in a given space (size, location, temperature)
- Performs adequately in the light provided
- Maintains output amid specific noise levels
- Operates unaffected by job-related odors

2. Domain: *Relationships*

Interpersonal: Relating to other people.
- Desires the company of, and interaction with, others
- Trusts others
- Interacts comfortably with peers, organizational superiors,

colleagues of lower status, external customers, suppliers, and other outside contacts
- Seeks agreement and compromise
- Empathizes with others
- Listens to others' experiences, ideas, and concerns
- Picks up non-verbal cues from others
- Sensitive to, but not ruled by, others' feelings
- Adjusts self-interests to the needs of others
- Demonstrates patience with others
- Respects the privacy of others
- Discloses own personal information discreetly and appropriately
- Cooperates
- Collaborates
- Negotiates with mutual gain in mind
- Values and respects others
- Treats every person as an individual
- Seeks input
- Supports colleagues
- Informs others appropriately and willingly
- Suggests
- Receives directives and corrections willingly
- Teaches
- Counsels
- Resolves conflict
- Strives to please others
- Honors confidences
- Works well as a member of a group

Influential: Asserting the self to move others.
- Inspires others
- Achieves through others
- Promotes ideas
- Persuades

Political: Functioning within an organization.
- Understands organizational purpose
- Operates using defined organizational structures

- Defers to organizational authority
- Performs through prescribed processes
- Submits personal will and needs to those of the organization
- Behaves in accord with generally accepted norms of the organization

Nurturing: Caring for and supporting others.
- Cares about others' well-being
- Serves others
- Comforts others
- Sustains others
- Heals others
- Guides others

3. Domain: *Performance Processes*

Mechanical: Working with things.
- Handles, makes, maintains, repairs, or assembles things
- Uses tools appropriately
- Operates equipment

Practical: Working according to accepted practices.
- Seeks to understand, focus on, and integrate customer requirements
- Strives for quality results
- Completes tasks
- Cares for tools and the work environment
- Attends to unpleasant but necessary work
- Creates structure, order, flow
- Employs consistent methods
- Follows prescribed procedures
- Seeks and implements improved processes without hesitation
- Performs repetitive work
- Initiates tasks
- Operates with little or no supervision, or, if appropriate, with constant or very frequent supervision
- Acts responsively
- Studies/considers before acting

Define the Job to Define Who You Hire 83

- Takes action swiftly
- Performs dependably
- Works at the correct level of detail, broadly conceptual or narrow and specific
- Delivers consistently
- Acts beyond job description; finds vacuums and fills them

Self-Management: Controlling one's work.
- Sets measurable goals
- Identifies factors central to success
- Plans activities
- Organizes work tasks for productivity
- Sorts and processes information from multiple channels
- Handles multiple, simultaneous tasks and assignments
- Resolves conflicting demands for resources
- Executes plans, coordinates efforts and resources
- Determines measures
- Complies with relevant information
- Assesses progress
- Tracks results
- Specifies budget
- Minimizes risk
- Inspects to assure adherence to specification
- Organizes resources for efficiency and effectiveness

Time: Functioning in relation to time.
- Exhibits promptness and punctuality
- Uses time efficiently
- Operates mindful of deadlines
- Draws motivation and stimulation from deadlines
- Can function at the appropriate pace
- Maintains a consistent pace
- Performs and endures for sustained periods
- Displays patience
- Studies the past
- Imagines the future

4. Domain: *Knowledge and Abilities*
Verbal: Communicating Through Words.

- Speaks a particular language to a specified standard
- Orally presents ideas to others in a clear manner
- Writes to a specified standard
- Comprehends additional language(s), if appropriate

Numerical: Understanding numbers and mathematics.
- Computes using arithmetic to a specified standard
- Performs high-level mathematics operations to a specified standard
- Perceives and comprehends quantitative relationships
- Estimates reasonably
- Measures accurately
- Budgets
- Forecasts

Sensory: Relating to the senses.
- Sees sharply
- Distinguishes color
- Smells keenly
- Tastes with acuity
- Touches adroitly
- Hears sharply and discerns tones

Spatial/Artistic: Comprehending, relating to, or working with representations of objects.
- Recognizes beauty and elegant design
- Conceives spatially balanced or pleasing compositions (for example, like a photographer or painter)
- Designs artistically
- Arranges with spatial sensitivity (for example, like a florist or interior decorator)
- Works with spatial adeptness (for example, like a moving truck loader, grocery sacker, or carpenter)
- Deciphers maps
- Comprehends models

Educational/Developmental: Learning information and skills.
- Demonstrates capacity to learn
- Reflects on and analyzes personal experiences for learning
- Exhibits inclination to learn

- Strives to develop own potential
- Seeks/welcomes new experiences and opportunities to learn on and off the job
- Solicits, accepts, and integrates feedback
- Asks for help
- Keeps skills current
- Improves skills, even after reaching a level of mastery
- Unlearns old ways and information that are obsolete
- Mentors others

Conceptual: Thinking about and generating ideas.
- Conceives new concepts
- Innovates
- Uniquely associates different, even disparate, ideas together
- Generates new possibilities that break the status quo
- Sees from a broad and fresh perspective
- Invents
- Develops and refines the ideas of others (for example, like an editor or manager)

Analytical: Thinking about the parts and their connections.
- Questions
- Clarifies and strives to simplify complexity
- Investigates
- Sorts and categorizes
- Translates
- Audits
- Researches
- Correlates
- Reviews
- Tests
- Diagnoses
- Solves problems
- Strategizes
- Decides

Technical: Knowing specific information and performing specific skills.
- Knows a body of special knowledge
- Applies special knowledge to a standard

- Demonstrates specific skill

Fiscal: Pertaining to financial matters.
- Consumes/deploys resources responsibly
- Spends within budget
- Devises ways to increase resource efficiency

Musical: Relating to music.
- Displays rhythm
- Grasps tonality, melody, and harmony
- Performs, composes, and arranges music

Natural: Interacting with the natural world.
- Displays comfort with and is knowledgeable about animals
- Is knowledgeable about plant life

The performance domains and capacities apply to work broadly. The work behaviors listed here only illustrate the possibilities. The particular work of a certain job may require many additional behaviors. In addition, many of the capacities and work behaviors listed above need a description of the standards that would more accurately describe them. For example, the physical capacity "Embodies strength" clearly needs further definition to describe it adequately (for example, "Embodies strength sufficient to lift and carry bulky thirty-pound packages for a distance of fifty feet," which would then be further described by the frequency and duration ratings).

A given capacity can include many behaviors that no one is likely to embody equally or even at all. A person may be capable of conceptualizing but not inventing, of relating empathetically to others but not really desiring many interactions with other people.

No work behavior within a capacity is absolute. All work behaviors essentially exist on a continuum. A certain range on that continuum will be more appropriate for one job than another. For example, the capacity curiosity lists a work behavior for challenging the status quo or convention. A high degree of this behavioral trait might desirable in a scientist working in research and development or a journalist in an investigative unit. In a data processing entry clerk or tax accountant, it might be counterproductive.

PUTTING IT ALL TOGETHER

To this point, you've had an overview of the concepts behind profiling a job. Now, let's look at a simple method for putting the process to work when you're ready to roll up your sleeves and profile the position.

The Job Profile Matrix, Figure 4-3 (page 88), provides a step-by-step process for listing the information illustrated in the process flow map shown in Figure 4-1. To complete it, simply begin filling in the blanks. List the job outcomes and the tasks that create them, the tasks' exceptional factors, and the capacities and work behaviors that enable task completion. Using the scales that appear above, assign ratings to each task for criticality, duration, and frequency, and assign each work behavior a minimum competency level for someone to be proficient in the job.

To get the most complete picture of a job's true nature, you might have a few different people profile the job, including incumbents, particularly those who perform the work extremely well, and supervisors responsible for the work. Compare notes and ratings. Discuss discrepancies to understand differing perspectives. The truer a picture of the position you draw, the more accurately you can hire someone to perform the job well.

ESSENTIALS

After completing the matrix (or filling in the blanks in the flow chart in Figure 4-1), you will have a thorough idea of what needs to be done in the job and what kind of person you need to do that work. So how do you typify the essential characteristics of a job so that you know what personal traits to seek in job applicants? Look at your ratings for criticality, frequency, and duration. Look at the competence ratings for the behaviors re-

Natural Selection Hiring Method™
Job Profile Matrix

Specific Job Outcome	Task(s) to Create Outcome	Task Criticality Rating	Task Duration Rating	Task Frequency Rating	Task's Exceptional Factors	Personal Capacities Required to Execute Task	Related Work Behaviors	Required Minimum Competency Level

Figure 4-3.

lated to the most critical, most frequent, and most sustained activities. Circle all the A ratings; these indicate what's truly important to doing the job. The more critical the task, the more frequent or longer in duration it is, and the greater its importance is to doing the job, the more important it becomes to match the job with a candidate with appropriate competencies.

After completing this exercise, you should be able to boil all the essentials down to complete the following sentence:

The kind of person who would most likely do well at performing this task would have qualities that include _____, _____, _____, and _____, because success at the job requires _____ .

This simple crystallization of the process gives you a good road map for the qualities you'll be seeking in applicants. The next chapter walks you through the process of evaluating applicants to assess their fit with your well-considered, well-defined needs.

A Word about Overkill

When you consider how complex many jobs really are, and how many different skills are involved in performing them well, it is little wonder that so many people simply default to hiring applicants with similar job experience. It is just easier to assume that they have the requisite competencies, although they very well may not.

The Natural Selection Method of Job Profiling and the four performance domains with their lists of capacities and multiple work behaviors may seem to be a complicated exercise merely to identify the qualities you would like to find in a new hire. But the output of this profiling process isn't at all overly complex for matching a person with a job in which you would like him or her to quickly become—and stay—productive. The method detailed here strikes a balance between ridiculously simple and ineffective and ridiculously complex and equally unworkable. It takes more than a moment, but doesn't require inordinate skills to complete. A thoughtful execution of the process detailed here should help you understand quite well the attributes you require in a person who is to excel at a given job.

The objective in going through this effort is for you to:
1. see, with a fresh pair of eyes, a job as a collection of work tasks organized by design;
2. see, perhaps for the first time, the not so readily visible but considerably important elements that make up a job; and
3. have a clear, well-considered basis for selecting people in no small part for their uniquely individual personal characteristics (which managers have been doing for a long time anyway, but with far less defensible rationales and methods).

True success in an extremely competitive market—where competition for workers is as keen as it is for customers—will come to those who take the time and make the effort to first identify the kind of people they need to achieve desired results, and then find and hire them.

Chapter Five

Predicting the Future by Sitting in Judgment

> You will get what you select for and lose what you don't.
>
> –Linda S. Gottfredson
> College of Human Resources
> University of Delaware

A television commercial for a chain of gigantic office products stores opens with a shot of a store manager at his desk quickly reviewing a thick catalog. He shakes his head, whistles, and says to himself, "Lowering prices...again."

Meanwhile, a young stock clerk is busy affixing stickers to stacks of merchandise. He reaches the final item, finishes with a flourish and a sigh, and announces, "And that's... the last... one!"

Just after the young man slaps on the last price sticker, the manager hands over that huge price list. "Here you go Willis, we've lowered prices again."

Stunned, the stocker stands there gawking.

Then, he shouts, "All right!" and begins jumping up and

down whooping with joy.

As the manager walks away, he shakes his head and declares, "That kid was a real find."

All employers should be so lucky with everyone they hire. How do you know when you've got a real find in that pool of applicants or line of interviewees?

When you decide to hire someone, you usually do it at the expense of hiring other available people. You make a judgment, based on the best information you can get, that the person you chose will perform as you expect. You are essentially predicting the future, prognosticating about the probability that your pick for the job will perform up to expectations.

In forming your judgment, making your prediction, you'll likely view candidates through a variety of lenses: their employment application or résumé, personal interviews, reference checks, perhaps formal competency tests, personality assessment instruments, computer-based tests, role playing, simulations involving videotaped scenarios, tryouts where candidates do the actual work, and perhaps even temporary work assignments or other try-before-you-buy methods. Many hiring managers assign great significance to face-to-face employment interviews, and they are, despite their shortcomings, central to the Natural Selection Hiring Method. We'll take up the subject of interviewing in Chapters 6 and 8; there is much to say about it.

No assessment instrument or technique is foolproof. Even "valid and reliable" assessment devices cannot guarantee that you'll get a good match between a high-scoring candidate and your requirements in terms of actual on-the-job performance. But the better informed you are about the choices you have and the best ways to use them, the more likely you are to make a good judgment and create a better future for your organization.

In this chapter, we'll look at the principles behind estimating an individual's suitability for a body of work. The next chapter provides the specific process for doing so.

In setting out to assess a job candidate, it's helpful first to step back from the process for a perspective check. Assessing suitability or even competence is not about finding the best person or even a good person for the job. The objective is to select someone who can fulfill the purpose of the task, delivering expected results in a desirable way. That's why you went through the drill of assigning criticality and competency ratings to tasks and behaviors in the job profile process. Even if you are very lucky, you are unlikely to hire anyone anywhere close to being perfect for executing the job responsibilities. You will be making inevitable tradeoffs. With accurate profiles of both the job and the available candidates, you will be in the desirable position of making wise decisions based on informed judgments as you settle on the candidate who is best suited to fulfilling the most important, if not all, aspects of the position.

PROBING QUESTIONS

In evaluating job candidates, you need the answers to some fundamental questions. Is this person:

- Capable (now or with some developmental help) of doing the job well enough?
- Willing to do the job well?
- Likely to do the job well?

An assessment process that can answer those questions first needs a positive response to each of these questions:

1. Do you know what you're looking for?
2. Do you have the means to recognize whether an applicant has the essential qualities you're seeking?
3. Will your assessments be accurate? Will they be valid?

You have the answer to the first question if you faithfully completed the job profile process in the previous chapter. As for the second, you need to know exactly what competence looks like, and you need to know you can test for it. You might recognize what you're looking for in a candidate but you're just as likely to miss it—or mistake false appearances for competence—without some structured assessment and evaluation procedures, which this book provides you with. Question three is perhaps the most vexing of all. And it's increasingly important because it's of increasing interest to government agencies and the courts, where applicants who feel discriminated against by unfair employment screening procedures turn for remedy.

Before we briefly explore the technical meanings of accuracy and validity in assessments, consider this analogy. I can absolutely prove to you that coping saws, miter boxes, and wood planes do not work as promised. In my hands they are neither accurate nor valid for their purposes. Similarly, psychologists can document that most employment interviews (along with many other screening methods) yield a low level of useful information with extremely limited accuracy in predicting future on-the-job work performance. Does this mean that no one should use either woodworking tools or employment interviews?

RELIABLY INVALIDATING VALIDITY

Assessing a person's capability and potential is an imprecise science, even when using state-of-the-art tools and techniques. Many factors come into play when you are trying to assess something as varied, complex, inconsistent, and unpredictable as the behavior of an individual human.

That said, here follow a few words about the principles of reliability and validity. An assessment (test, instrument, or procedure) is reliable to the extent to which it is consistent in reaching a conclusion or providing a judgment about a person across time and situations. In other words, if you take a test on Monday morning of this week in Boston, and the same test on Friday afternoon a month from now in Sydney, Australia, the results should basically, if not completely, be the same. The assessment is reliable if it delivers dependably consistent results. Because it is consistent, however, doesn't mean it is necessarily the least bit accurate. Recall the old joke about a broken clock being right twice a day.

Enter validity. A valid assessment is one that measures what it's supposed to be measuring. A valid assessment yields a measure that is appropriate for the purpose. For example, say you're trying to measure the dimensions of a house. A sophisticated, industrial-sized metal measuring tape is a more valid assessment instrument for this task than either an elastic tape or a child's little ruler. The elastic tool would probably yield both inaccurate and inconsistent information. The cheap ruler would be off the mark because the device is not particularly precise and using the tiny instrument to measure such a large area presents multiple opportunities for errors in calculating the measurement.

To accurately measure human qualities, many psychological instruments, including some that are used to screen potential employees, must first go through rigorous testing to establish their reliability and validity. In developing a test, sample questions are administered to as many as thousands of individuals in field studies, and the results are analyzed by measurement experts. The prospective test must prove to give the same accurate results time after time and to be equally applicable to all groups (such as age groups and ethnic minority populations) who take it for it to be deemed fair. Creating or revising a comprehensive achievement, aptitude, personality, or intelligence test can, according to the Association of Test Publishers based in Washington, DC, easily cost several million dollars.

While we will look at employment testing in considerable detail in Chapter 7, it's worth noting here that most assessment methods used in most organizations are not certifiable as either reliable or valid. To assess the likelihood of a person performing well in a new job is to prejudge his or her future actions, putting you squarely into the realm of the unquantifiable, unprovable, and unknowable. You simply cannot be certain about any prediction of any individual's future behavior. People are not static, measurable objects, and they don't live in the sealed, controlled environment of a laboratory. So you simply cannot make judgments about a human that are going to be either completely valid or completely reliable—that's axiomatic. Nonetheless, you can make judgments that are informed, reasonable, and defensible.

Most hiring managers and even most recruiting and hiring specialists in the human resources departments of large organizations are not psychologists. Nothing in this book is intended to try to turn you into one. We will focus on some methods that will help to inform you more fully about the candidates you are considering, so that you can have a far more reasoned basis for your guess about someone's future performance.

JUDGMENT AND DESIGNER-LABEL BIAS

Everyone assesses others. Most of us do it unconsciously almost all the time. Our culture embraces and celebrates opinions and judgments. For proof of this, turn on any talk radio show, or think about the first question most of us inevitably ask our partner or kids when we see them upon arriving home: How was your day today? We ask for and receive a judgment. Ask a friend if he's seen the latest movie. If he has, the odds are that he'll answer not with a simple yes or no but with his assessment of the flick ("It was great/terrible/OK").

We form impressions and make judgments regarding people's dress, their words, tone of voice, the way they walk, look us in the eye, shake our hand, and so on. Some managers place a high value on such casual assessments and unabashedly use them as a prime basis for hiring. Others work hard to consciously suppress their instinctive biases about such trivialities, knowing they can color one's judgment about more substantive matters such as one's competence to perform a job.

An assessment error that may be far less apparent than even the subtle prejudices most of us recognize in ourselves is the assessment by label fallacy. This is where someone evaluates a job candidate (or a colleague at performance review

Predicting the Future by Sitting in Judgment

time) by thinking about and assessing the person in terms of labels rather than behaviors. For example, a manager might pass judgement on the value of someone's customer focus, change management, communication skills, or teamwork. What is being assessed when someone judges these nouns, these labels? To one person, teamwork may mean functioning in a way that's spontaneous, highly collaborative, and somewhat loosely structured, like a basketball team, while to another person, teamwork could imply a rigid, highly defined, hierarchical way of functioning, more like a football team. Without knowing precisely what one means by teamwork, assessing for it is virtually impossible. To assess accurately, as you will see explained in much greater detail later, you need to know what you're looking for, specify how you're going to test for it, and define what it looks like so you know when you've found it.

Would any two people give the same definition for the broad terms we're using here? How can one make judgments about competence if its definition is ambiguous? You cannot assess someone in terms of a specific term or label. In evaluating a prospective hire (or a colleague who is up for a raise), you can only assess behaviors and their outcomes. These behaviors, of course, need to be specified.

Some behavior descriptors, such as coaching, developing direct reports, and managing projects, sound good but tell you little more than noun labels do. Such "action-sounding" terms are broad, imprecise, and open to wide interpretation. When you assess for a capacity, you need to evaluate at a fine level of detail. Only by looking at specific actions can you project to the broader capacities encompassed by broadly sweeping labels.

Similarly, some managers confuse indicators with performance. Because a car comes with a speedometer that measures a top speed of 140 miles per hour doesn't mean that the car can actually drive that fast. The speedometer is merely an indicator; actual performance may vary. In the same sense, "behavioral profiling instruments" (such as the Myers-Briggs Type Indicator, or any of the many DISC-type behavioral-style instruments) are only indicators (and only self-indications at that, having come from one's own assessment of oneself rather than from any actual observed behavior).

People familiar with such behavioral indicators may refer to others or themselves with the labels conferred by these popular devices that, in effect, categorize people. "She's an INTJ and he's a high D; they'll never get along."

Such categorizations of behavioral preferences can be dangerous shorthand that imparts broad assumptions about a person's actual behaviors while specifying little about true capacity to fill a position. Behavioral patterns are like weather patterns. Knowing the season or even the month doesn't tell you what the weather is going to be like today.

Knowing someone's general behavioral orientation (as a decisive, make-it-happen bottom-liner; a fearful, rule-bound stickler for details; an analytical and judgmental introvert; a driven-to-persuade, big-picture extrovert; a low-key and easy-going worker; and so on) does not tell you who someone is either as a person or as a work performer. A behavioral profile summary can tell you neither how someone has performed in the past nor how he or she will perform in the future.

In the same vein, many people wrongly assume that particular attitudes or behavioral styles, whether they are labels or not, translate into success in performing certain work. Rejecting an apparently quiet and unassuming person for a sales post because he or she doesn't immediately appear to be gregarious can be a most unfortunate, self-defeating act. Gabby sycophants may appear to be born salespeople. But rather than persuading customers (whom they may well put off) to part with more dollars, their manner may have the exact opposite effect. In any profession, people who defy the stereotype may actually be more effective and more competent, and may produce better results, than those who typify it.

A similar disabling labeling occurs when you say that you want to hire someone "just like Juanita." Everyone shed a tear the day she left the firm; she was so nice, so interested in helping wherever she could, and a superb baker to boot. She had to be the best bookkeeper on the planet. You're not going to find another bookkeeper like her. Actually, you shouldn't try. When you assess candidates using the list of critical capacities and behaviors for the post (described in the previous chapter), you might end up hiring someone very different from Juanita. If you hire someone who seems just like her, the new jobholder may still be loved by all but fail to do the job.

THE CURSE OF THE KNOWING EYE

One of the paradoxes about assessing people is that your very experience as a manager may be a liability when you size up an applicant. Experience with people often gives you insight into them; you learn to draw inferences from subtleties and small amounts of information. The secret to successful assessment is to see not what appears to be there but to see what may not be apparent to the undisciplined eye.

People being evaluated for a job—in an interview or performing in a simulation—know that they are under scrutiny and may act quite differently than they normally would on the job. They may sound like they know more than they do or less than they do. They may appear more animated (from nervous tension, perhaps) or more withdrawn (from fear of "blowing" the opportunity) than they really are.

Having gone to the trouble of carefully identifying the personal characteristics you want in a jobholder only to casually assess them by superficial impressions is as big a mistake as falling prey to the skill-fill fallacy mentioned in Chapter 1. You're cheating yourself by not ascertaining to the greatest degree you can whether you have someone who's really capable of doing the job in the way you want it done. Overlooking or failing to recognize someone's suitability to adequately fill a job may deny a "qualified" candidate (see Chapter 2) a job offer. That might cost you a lawsuit. But it also may well deny you a talented and tremendously productive resource.

Assess or Else!

In assessing an individual candidate's appropriateness for a given position, you need to rate him or her on each critical capacity and work behavior. Don't make the classic error of associating a few apparent traits with an overall capability to do the job. That can be a fatally dangerous leap.

For example, if you were to consider me for a customer service position with your company, you probably would like my marketing background, my verbal ability, problem-solving skills, and genuine dedication to customer satisfaction. You might give me the job and think you got a bargain even when I talked you into paying me more salary than you budgeted. And you would probably be making a colossal mistake.

Here's why. As you saw in our meetings before you made the job offer, I'm adept at social interaction. But only in fairly small doses—it's an intentionally acquired, not innate, skill for me. My inclinations run toward alternating person-to-person interactions with more solitary work. If I spend too much time with other people I become ornery—not the best disposition for someone charged with pleasing your customers. Moreover, the necessarily well-defined policies and procedures your company so thoughtfully crafted to guide customer transactions and interactions would start to chafe me. Formal structure feels confining, even stifling, to me. I would break the rules—not to start trouble, but because I would honestly feel it was the right thing to do. I would start dreaming up and proposing new methods, new procedures, and new policies to improve your company, which is something I genuinely like to do. When, for probably very good reasons, you would respectfully decline most (if not all) of my earnest suggestions, I would become demotivated.

My sick days would increase. My complaining to coworkers would begin to affect morale. I would start looking for ways to quietly fight back with some not-so-apparent passive aggressive techniques. I would follow the rules absolutely precisely, even to the detriment of customer goodwill. So what, I don't care anymore, I would think. I would withdraw. I would watch the clock and count down the minutes until lunch. I would do nothing that was not specified in the job description. At the weekly team meeting, I would sit silently with arms folded, refusing to say a word even during the brainstorming portion that I used to love so. Every time someone made a positive comment, I would mutter sarcastic comments under my breath. And on and on until you would curse the day you hired me, the day you were so impressed by the "perfect" fit between your requirements and my obvious skills.

My résumé, my enthusiasm, and your gut all told you, "Hire this guy now!" All that was missing was a structured assessment process that would have raised the yellow flags, planted the seeds of doubt, and given you an opportunity to avoid the misery you would have endured until I found another job or you completed the mountain of paperwork to build the case for a clean firing. And while you're frittering away precious managerial time doing that, you're also wasting more time frantically trying to retrofit your wayward employee—desperately attempting to coach, encourage, and inspire better performance from that guy who, just a few short months ago, seemed so wonderfully promising.

Assess for what you truly need from the employee.

ASSORTMENT OF ASSESSMENTS

The challenge in assessing another person is to get past impressions, labels, and assumptions. Know what qualities you seek—do the analysis that defines the personal capacities that are most critical to producing the desired results—and then rigorously and open-mindedly test and judge for those qualities.

You have many options beyond the time-honored employment interview for assessing and judging the fitness of your would-be colleagues. There is a staggering number of commercially available employment tests (paper and pencil or high-tech) that claim to do everything from indicating whether an applicant has a drug problem to judging an applicant's mechanical ability (see Chapter 7 for a thorough review). In addition to those familiar filters, there are many other techniques for separating the hopeful from the employed.

> An assessment is a comprehensive, multifaceted analysis; it must be judgment-based and personal.
> –Grant Wiggins
> President of the Center on Learning, Assessment, and School Structure

On the job. One of the most powerful assessment options is the real thing: watching the candidate doing the job. The most valid and reliable predictor of job performance is job performance. That's why sports recruiters don't hire off a résumé; they travel to watch their quarry in action. Law firms that cross swords with worthy opponents sometimes hire their fiercest adversaries. Executives who meet at an industry trade convention watch their counterparts in action, some with a recruiter's eye. Savvy sales managers who spot talent on a car dealer's showroom floor, or sense it in a telemarketer calling them, sometimes turn the tables and start pitching career opportunities. Keeping an eye open for gracious, prompt service in restaurants, retail establishments, and the like can help you find service-minded employees who have, to a much greater degree than candidates lying anonymously in a pile of résumés, proven their worth.

If you don't find the people you need in the world at large through serendipity, ask candidates from the résumé pile to let you watch them work. Invite them; pay them to work for a day or two at your place, doing as much of the real work of their prospective new job as is practical.

"Context and the real work environment are much better

predictors than interviews or any other candidate assessment," says America Works, Inc. president Lee Bowes, who did her Ph.D. at Harvard on employment issues. In the late 1980s, Bowes wrote a book about how poorly most organizations do their hiring. Today she heads a company that places oftentimes unskilled welfare recipients with little or no job experience into jobs in several major U.S. cities.

There's no substitute, she says, for people getting the sense of the job and the workplace on location. "Many times," she reports, "candidates who spend a couple of days or even a few hours on a job will say, 'this isn't for me.' That saves both the employee and the employer the time and aggravation of a hiring mistake." And it increases the odds of success even for the hardcore unemployed. Some 85 percent of the welfare recipients placed by America Works who make it through the critical first four months at a job are still there a year later.

Ask an applicant to try out for the job. Hiring someone to wash cars? Ask him to wash a car according to your directions, or with another member of your staff. If the candidate has ten years of car washing experience but cannot—or more likely will not—do it as directed, he is not qualified. Conversely, if the applicant has never touched a sponge before but pays attention to instructions and ably follows another employee's example, he may be extremely well qualified.

Free samples. An applicant for a financial analyst position who currently holds such a job might come to an interview with samples of reports he or she has prepared. Likewise, a teacher might bring sample lesson plans. A bricklayer or landscaper's helper looking for similar work might present photos of jobs he or she has worked on. Such samples, in the nomenclature of employment specialists, are known as work product. When someone comes with a little show-and-tell presentation, it demonstrates pride in his or her work.

There are a few things to bear in mind about such apparently helpful shortcuts to determining technical competence. Such samples (forming a collection of what presumably is the candidate's best work) are what we term in the next chapter *represented* competence. You don't know the circumstances under which they were created or the applicant's role in producing what they are presenting as their work, although you can ask about that directly. (The best way is to ask, "What was your exact role in the creation of this particular piece? Please walk me through the process from concept to execution.")

Marveling at an applicant's great work products can potentially blind a hiring manager to the candidate's other flaws. If you fall in love with the idea of this person producing this work for you, remember that the person comes along with that work. Stick to your script in assessing and valuing all the important capacities for the job, in addition to the technical knowledge and skills.

Not every applicant may have work products to show you. That doesn't necessarily mean that he or she is not as qualified as ones who do. It could be that they produce—or are capable of producing—work that is every bit as good or better. Perhaps they even work more consistently and more pleasantly. Use every means to fairly and fully assess all your leading candidates to get as balanced and complete a picture as you can, so that you can make the best judgment possible.

Look at work samples with critical eyes that are open to their limitations and potential drawbacks.

Auditions. Let's say you want to hire an art director to design ads for your ad agency. You might look at a candidate's portfolio. As you page through the beautiful samples in the nice presentation binder, you could ask the applicant to design an ad from words already written (copy, in ad parlance).

If you ask an applicant to create an ad (or some other work sample), there are several important considerations to bear in mind:

- Your "test" should apply to all applicants who've reached this stage in the screening process, and be identically administered to all. (You want to have equivalent information about all of them, and you surely want to be fair to all.)
- You need to decide what supplies you'll provide, and what work space they'll use.

- Is there a time limit?
- How will you assess the quality of what the applicant delivers to you? By what measures will you and others evaluate competence? Will you have a formal rating scale, and keep a record of your judgments?
- Your assessment might include process as well as final outcome. For example, the ideal applicant you seek might be one who wants to meet the marketing objectives of your ad agency's clients, not just create pretty pieces of art. So an applicant who asks about client objectives, other client ads that may already be running, the company's history, the competitive situation, and the like might well be more valuable to the agency than another candidate who creates aesthetically pleasing works of art that exist in a vacuum, without relevance.

When you can observe a prospective employee on the job, doing actual work, you see him or her in context—removed from the "let me sell you on myself" mode of many other employment assessment situations. Your judgments about the applicant are therefore far more informed, relevant, and valid.

Other try-before-you-buy methods include hiring temporary workers (they're now available from temporary help agencies in virtually every profession: accounting, law, medicine, marketing, computing, and so on), or extending the courting and evaluation period by hiring a prospective hire as a consultant on a project.

Then there's the classic but oft-overlooked trial or probationary period, without question the most valid, tangibly job-related, and useful assessment method. In this method, the person is an employee working in the actual position, in your culture. You can really see what you're getting. This superb assessment method isn't used as much as it should be because it requires a rigorous system to work properly.

First, you need to make the conditional nature of this evaluation period absolutely clear to the employee. (Work with your employment lawyer to craft the necessary wiggle verbiage so that when the probationary period ends, you have not implied a contract for permanent employment. Couch the assignment as a temporary, demonstration period with a well-defined, no-later-than-X termination point, at which time you may offer the employee regular employment.)

During the trial period, intensely and formally scrutinize the new recruit's performance helpfully, thoroughly, and bluntly. Use formal written evaluations to detail performance achievement and deficiencies. If the employee clearly isn't going to cut it, cut your losses sooner rather than later. The candidate may well realize the same thing you do. Why prolong the agony, or raise false expectations for a longer tenure?

The Ultimate Act of Assessment and Selection

In my presentations to management groups, I often speak of leadership and productivity. Central to both is an uncommon yet profoundly important managerial act: firing under-productive employees. Firing people who are not performing—oftentimes because they simply are not suited to their work—frequently has the effect of boosting both productivity and morale. In many cases the coworkers of departed colleagues knew, probably long before management figured it out, that the employee was not pulling his or her share of the load, that he or she was indirectly, if not directly, increasing the burden on everyone else or making them feel like fools for working as hard as they did for little or no greater reward.

Firing is an extension of hiring. To carefully assess someone's qualifications and capabilities before they join the payroll only to ease up on the monitoring once they have is silly and self-defeating.

Most managers simply wait too long to do the deed. Some simply ignore the problem and hope that it will resolve itself (it usually won't). Others try rescuing, coaching, threatening, coaxing, inspiring, and all manner of retrofitting techniques on the errant employee before doing what needs to be done. They waste their time and that of many others in the process.

People working in a job in which they cannot be successful are suffering. They are disappointed in themselves, feel guilty for not working to expectation, and live with the agonizing torture of waiting for you to do what they cannot do for themselves—pull the plug on the misery. When that fateful time comes, almost without exception in my own experience (and this is confirmed by thousands of other managers), the emotion that appears in the eyes of someone whom we have decided to let go after fair and careful consideration is not surprise, anger, or even sadness. It is relief.

After almost every presentation in which I mention firing as a positive managerial act, some of the attendees approach me and thank me for giving them the permission and inspiration to go back to their office and do what they have been avoiding.

Dismissing people who are not producing to expectation is the ultimate act of selection.

Almost the real thing. If you can't have an applicant audition by doing the exact job duties in your operation, and you can't reasonably watch them do something similar somewhere else, you still can approach that ideal of candidate assessment.

As an old Spanish proverb points out, it is one thing to talk of bulls, it is another to enter the bullring. One way you can put your good-sounding candidate into the ring is to have him participate in a simulation—a reasonable approximation of the actual job (or some important component of it). During World War II, the U.S. Office of Strategic Services (the CIA's predecessor) wanted to assess candidates to be OSS agents, or spies. "Tell me about yourself," didn't have high validity in predicting success in this unusual and high-stakes line of work. The OSS created a number of assessment tests, including realistic high-stress situations, to simulate the conditions and pressure in which a wartime spy might find himself. These simulations included playing a role during intense interrogation without cracking, engaging in wilderness survival, memorizing a map, staying on task during difficult circumstances, dealing with an incompetent colleague, and so on.

These then-experimental procedures created by government psychologists turned out to be quite reliable in predicting actual performance. There were two reasons for their success. First, the assessments were based on context; they related directly to the application of skills that the candidates would need to be successful on the job. Second, the wide battery of assessments dealt with the job holistically. Not everyone was good at everything, but candidates were able to demonstrate the breadth and depth of their capacities in a way that no traditional testing could assess.

Today, the successor to the Army's holistic assessment procedures is the assessment center. Some large organizations maintain what in essence are work laboratories for simulating what are usually managerial- or executive-level work situations. The classic example is the "in-box test," where a managerial candidate is observed working his or her way through the in-box at a desk in a faux office.

Behind a one-way mirror, evaluators note how the subject organizes the work, delegates, handles ambiguity, resolves conflicting priorities, and so on. Assessment center exercises may include report writing, orally presenting a proposal to other executives, and role-playing. Evaluators thus observe a candidate's information gathering process, problem-solving techniques, capacity to prioritize, approach to functioning as part of a team, decision-making methods, and the like.

Of course, evaluating performance across the wide range of skills ostensibly being tested in such an artificial setting is open to interpretation. Still, assessment centers can be a way of identifying managerial talent that otherwise might not have the opportunity to bubble up or be noticed.

The controlled work simulation concept has application in manufacturing situations as well. Toyota and General Motors put aspiring assembly workers at their joint plant in California through exercises to test skills for problem-solving, following instructions, and working with colleagues as part of a team. (Human resource consulting firm Development Dimensions International has made a specialty of designing such simulations, and brags that it uses the assessment center concept for both hiring and developing its own employees. With offices all around the world, you can contact DDI in Bridgeville, Pennsylvania, at (412) 257-2277. Their Web site is www.ddiworld.com and their e-mail address is info@ddiworld.com.)

You may not have an elaborate assessment center at your disposal, but you can have a candidate participate in a scenario. Want to know how someone who says all the right things about teamwork really works as part of a team? Set up a team-based interaction. Team skills are visible, so they are observable and assessable. You can see how someone participates in a discussion, yields to others, considers others' ideas, negotiates, volunteers, and so on. You can ask your applicant to play the role of the position for which he or she is being considered. Simulate a team meeting where the group is being asked to reach a decision, share information, set a schedule, name a product, or whatever you want. Inject some conflict by having someone feign confusion over the candidate's suggestions or introducing a personality clash. Observe behaviors that will indicate something about the candidate's communication skills, self-confidence, politeness, assertiveness, creativity, analytical skill, ability to focus on tasks, or even commitment to customer satisfaction (for example, does the candidate mention or ask about customer requirements during the group's discussion or decisions?).

High tech. Naturally, in today's electronically charged world, assessments also come in gee-whiz versions. The principle of the airline pilot's realistic flight simulator is now being applied in other professions thanks to videotapes, laser discs, and computers. For example, in testing command officers who want to be promoted in fire departments, videotaped vignettes challenge the officers' knowledge and judgment. A series of "What would you do here?" scenarios representing several real-world situations are used to assess knowledge of structures, equipment deployment, command decisions, and so on. While technological solutions can be a quantum leap toward realism from the insular sterility of paper-and-pencil exams, they still tend to be weak surrogates for the pressured, frenetic nitty-gritty of reality.

As advances in technology promise to close the gap between on-the-job reality and electrically induced virtual reality, simulations for assessments will likely grow in both validity and popularity.

Voyeurism. Even though you may not be able to watch a candidate "doing his thing," you can have him or her watch your colleagues doing theirs. Have your leading candidates spend a day or two in your operations doing a "job shadow." That's where they spend a part or all of a day with someone who does the same or a similar job, or interact with the people they would work with in the event they took the job, or just spend time in the workplace generally watching what goes on there all day. As Lee Bowes points out, there's no better way to get a feel for the workplace than by spending time in it.

Ann Rhoades, executive vice president of Promus Hotels (which includes several major brands such as Doubletree Hotels, Hampton Inns, Homewood Suites, and others), says that at some properties, candidates for a housekeeper's job have their employment interview in a hotel room bathroom as someone actually cleans the toilet. "We let them know right away what the job's really all about, and some people just walk right out," she says.

Despite the occasional abruptly terminated interview, this method of putting the candidate immediately into the true job environment and many other innovations that Ann and her colleagues employ help to secure employees who are willing to do the jobs they are applying for. In a very tight labor market, where competition for people is intense, some hotels in the Promus group have virtually no turnover and haven't had an opening in years.

Everyone acts in response to his or her environment. Behavior on the job is a constant dance of action and reaction. No matter how good a job your recruiting materials do in describing your company, no matter how thorough your description of the work environment and the team members, there's no comparison between description and experience. For the prospective employee, an hour spent watching the real job environment may beat five spent listening to abstract descriptions of it.

He says, she says. If a résumé is a sales brochure, then references are testimonial endorsements—if you can get anyone to talk with you at all about a candidate. By all means, check references! Have applicants sign a release giving you their express permission to ask others about them and gather relevant information about their employment background (tell them, "It really helps us to better understand your qualifications").

Go one step further. Enlist the applicant in assisting your reference-gathering effort. Encourage them to gather current phone numbers and to call their own references to ask them to make time for you and provide you with information. Words said about someone you've barely met by someone you don't know could be either gossipy hearsay or expert testimony. You need to get as many insights as you can, especially any related to the critical capacities required by the job. Ask references to specifically address those qualities.

Ask the candidate's references to give you the names of other people they know who also know the candidate. Work that B list and develop a C list. The truth is out there. W.L. Gore & Associates (a high-tech chemical and fabrics maker) seeks up to ten references for each new hire. A former airline executive told me that reference checks by peers of the potential hire are much more successful in digging up dirt. They get a peer-to-peer conversation going and the truth comes tumbling out. "We found out all kinds of things about candidates that a professional reference checker in HR or hiring manager never would have when pilots checked on other pilots."

You can't be too careful these days. Workplace violence aside, there are, as the president of a large multinational trade association once suggested to me, "many people in the workforce today who wouldn't ordinarily even be considered employable if the labor market weren't so tight." So check and double-check.

When you hit a brick wall of resistance from a reference who is mouthing the company line about divulging no more than his or her former colleague's name, rank, and employee ID number, try this ploy devised by Bob Losyk, a former human resources manager who gives seminars on hiring. He suggests a most subtle and effective maneuver to pierce this protective veil: guilt. Tell the reference, "I'm about ready to offer Carlos a job but I can't without a little more information about him. He told me you could help..."

This flip on the old gambit of "come on, I'd save you from hiring a bad employee if I could" catches people off guard and appeals to their better selves. Of course if all else fails you can always resort to the cut-to-the-chase bottom-line: "Just one quick question, then. Would you hire him to work with you again?"

Keep notes on your conversations. Conflicting information is to be expected; not everybody will be scrupulously honest and forthcoming. If you get only negative reports, including those from the references the candidate provided you, then obviously something's not right. Even if your candidate can explain it all away, caveat emptor.

Chapter Six

Assessing Applicants: A Process

> Absent a judgment by individuals or groups who are knowledgeable, it is simply not possible to tell whether a task has been executed satisfactorily or in an exemplary fashion.
>
> —Howard Gardner,
> Author, Multiple Intelligences

Like everything else in the Natural Selection Hiring Method, success in assessing your candidates depends on executing a process, shown in Figure 6-1 (page 114). You've already profiled the job and determined the personal capacities you'd like to find in your new hire by following the process detailed in Chapter 4.

Before selecting someone to join your payroll, you need to assess how well he or she meets your criteria. In making that assessment, you are making a judgment about the candidate, deeming him or her fit (or unfit) to achieve specific objectives by performing a set of tasks in a desirable way.

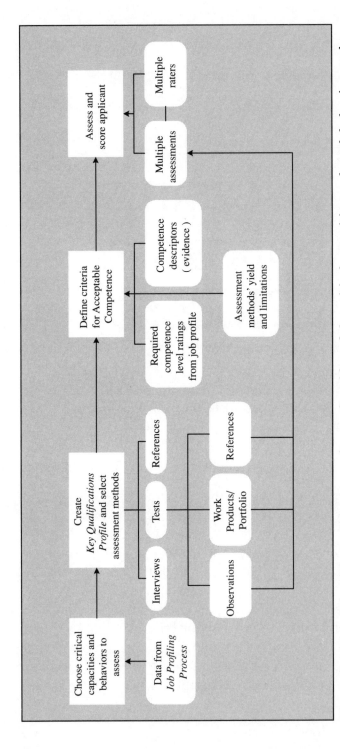

Figure 6-1. Assessing job candidates requires a clear idea of the critical capacities and work behaviors to be assessed, multiple appropriate assessment methods, a specified level for the competence required to do the job, a clear definition of what constitutes that competence, an understanding of the degree to which your assessment procedures indicate that competence, and multiple assessors sharing common criteria and methods by which to evaluate the candidate.

DEFINING THE DESIRABLE

To assess your candidates, you need guidelines so that you can —by assessing and scoring—consider each one in a consistent and fair manner. That helps you collect good information that will help you make a better informed decision about whom you should make the job offer to. Grant Wiggins, who has a doctorate in education from Harvard, specializes in performance assessments. In his 1998 book *Educative Assessments*, he suggests that an effective scoring guide answers the following questions:

- By what criteria should performance be judged?
- Where should we look and what should we look for to judge performance success?
- What does the range in the quality of performance look like?
- How do we determine validly, reliably, and fairly what score should be given and what that score means?
- How should the different levels of quality be described and distinguished from one another?

Wiggins suggests that "a performance standard is established by agreeing on specific, worthy samples of work that meet a valid target." So if you specify that your applicant needs to know how to be a good hole driller, you need to know what well-drilled holes look like by having some such holes—or worthy proxies such as pictures, diagrams, or descriptions—for comparison. You also need to know how you're going to apply that standard to assess candidates for their drill skills. Will you give them a written test that asks about drills and holes? Interview them to ascertain what they know and how they feel about drilling? Ask them to bring in samples of holes they've drilled? Watch finalists drill holes in your shop? Constructing a guideline and following the assessment process helps you to determine an appropriate method that you can apply consistently to all candidates.

To specify what you are going to assess for in your candidate evaluations, you'll create a Key Qualifications Profile (KQP), explained in detail below, that spells out a standard for performance against which you can assess job candidates.

Before you can determine assessment measures, you need to precisely specify what exactly you're going to assess in your job candidates. Begin by reviewing your Job Profile for the position. Focus on the ratings with high scores for criticality, duration, and competence level required in all the job behaviors from all the capacities you listed as applying to this position. You likely will not be able to assess all the important characteristics you'd like to find in your ideal new employee. By reviewing your ratings for the most important qualities for job success, decide which ones you will actually evaluate candidates on. As tempting as it may be to try to assess for everything you'd like to find in your ideal candidate, you need to limit the field for three important reasons:

1. to properly focus the assessment so that you can construct valid measures for the most vital components that are valid and reliable,
2. to assess each candidate in an identical manner (if you don't you can't accurately compare one with another, and you may run afoul of equal employment opportunity laws), and
3. to allocate a reasonable allotment of time for preparing and executing assessments (you could not possibly spend the time to prepare assessments for all the important factors, much less complete them competently for all the prospects you'll review).

Force yourself to make the tough calls. If you're stuck trying to strike a balance between the three importance factors, you might rank criticality as most important, duration next, and then frequency. Don't be surprised if there is a great discrepancy between the ratings assigned to a given task's criticality and the amount of time someone spends on it.

Consistent with Pareto's 80/20 principle, a very large percentage of what any of us do on the job probably isn't nearly as important as those critical contributions we make every so often. Since you have to choose what you're going to assess, isolate those factors that you really need to be sure your new employee has. Here's a simple test for choosing: Focus on the qualities that are so important that the job simply could not be done if they were missing in the jobholder.

Remember that you get what you assess for. If it's truly important, assess for it. If you don't, you leave it to chance, fate, or accident that you'll end up with the kind of person you really want.

CREATING THE KEY QUALIFICATIONS PROFILE

To begin the assessment process, construct a Key Qualifications Profile by following the format outlined in Figure 6-2 on page 118.

In building the Key Qualifications Profile, you construct the basis for the following:

1. determining whether a candidate has the qualities and degree you've determined are important for this position,
2. specifying what constitutes evidence of having a particular quality, and
3. describing the basis to determine the extent to which a candidate possesses a desired quality.

The capacity/behavior column contains those critical characteristics that you've determined, from the Job Profiling Process described in Chapter 4, are most important to successfully doing the job. The competence level was also determined in the job profile exercise. List the choice for the level that you made from the scale

- Mastery
- Advanced Competence
- Competent
- Developmental

and then go on to the next column to describe what exactly you intend that level of competence to mean—what it is and how you would recognize whether a candidate had it. Ideally,

Natural Selection Hiring Method™		
Key Qualifications Profile		
Capacity/ Behavior	Required Competence Level	Demonstrated by...
1.		
2.		
3.		
etc.		

Figure 6-2. A Key Qualifications Profile describes the characteristics desired in a job candidate, and specifies in detail what constitutes each characteristic and the evidence by which one can determine whether and to what extent the applicant has that quality.

you would have a thorough, detailed description of what each level of competence means in terms of skills or behavior. That would represent the full continuum of a skill path from novice to master, which can be a superb tool for employee development.

However, for our hiring purposes you are specifying the minimum level of skills that you would accept because that's the minimum level required to do the job as you've determined it needs to be done. (In this part of the process, you're deciding to hire someone only if they have a given level of competence for a specific, vitally important capacity to do an important part of the job.)

In the *Demonstrated by...* column, you describe the evidence you need in order to know whether someone has or doesn't have the quality to the standard you want. You're essentially completing the following sentence: *This competence at an acceptable level would be evidenced by...*

To write a description of an appropriate "test" for a specific trait (knowledge of something, ability to demonstrate a skill, or desirable behavior) in a candidate, answer this question: "If I could see a person exhibiting this quality or performing this action at the desired level of competence, what would they be doing?" Alternatively, ask, "What would be evidence that this person has the desired quality or engages in the desired behavior?" Essentially, you are describing how you will "know it when you see it."

For example, let's say you are hiring someone to ride a bicycle in a parade. A critical behavior in this case is the ability to ride a two-wheeled bike (a physical capacity from the personal domain). The competence level required is advanced competent, which means, as defined in the *Demonstrated by...* column:

> *Progressively passing three successive levels of difficulty on the test track. Level one—unassisted, the applicant successfully pedals two laps of the track without incident. Level two—applicant successfully negotiates the standard configuration of obstacles without knocking over a single cone, bumping a barrier, losing control of the cycle, or falling. The applicant may make up to three attempts to complete the obstacle course successfully. Upon successful completion, the applicant completes the course again in no more than two attempts. Level three—the applicant successfully negotiates the obstacle course while visibly smiling and waving. Following an initial successful run, the applicant successfully completes the course in this manner again in no more than two attempts.*

This description defines what the required level of competence for the task is and how it would be evidenced. Another critical physical capacity might be *stamina*, which could be defined at the competent level as *completing, without stopping, ten laps on the test track in no more than ten minutes while ex-*

hibiting no signs of being winded or suffering undue fatigue or physical distress.

So far, this is straightforward. Physical capacities tend to be easily defined. Let's move into less visible capacities from the personal domain, namely demonstrating appropriate attitudinal, emotional, and ethical capacities for the job. You don't want your new employee terrorizing little children along the parade route with daredevil bike tricks! How can you describe this competence and what would be evidence of it?

First, let's describe the capacities, not as labels, as in the previous chapter, but in terms of desirable specifics:

> *...presenting a calm, relaxed demeanor; when executing test rides, candidate does so at an appropriate speed; at all times, candidate is visibly in control of the bike with at least one hand on the handlebars, riding seated and upright, maintaining a prudent pace, making no unnecessary maneuvers, and taking no unnecessary risks; exhibits no "hot dogging"—showing off, testing the limits, or demonstrative bragging about bike handling prowess; and faithfully follows all test instructions, perhaps asking questions to ensure understanding.*

Such behaviors would give an indication of the qualities you seek—a respectful attitude, attention and deference to instructions, a mature and responsible approach to the job, an appropriate display of personal passion, and emotional stability with self-control, and no inappropriate displays of personal feelings. (All these behavioral descriptors are derived directly from the performance domains taxonomy in Chapter 4.) As you may have noticed, evidence for observing some of these intangibles is in the form of what the candidate does not do; in other words, the candidate may define a low-risk orientation by *not* exhibiting high-risk behavior.

Bear in mind that an observably well mannered, deferential biker might not be whom he appears to be. The candidate could be a shrewd faker, intentionally presenting the kind of calm, careful behavior he assumed you'd be looking for.

That's why, as mentioned previously, good assessment

does not rely on a single measure. Just as a doctor doesn't diagnose a malady simply by taking someone's temperature, you can't judge a candidate with a single assessment method. By employing several different, appropriate measures, none of which is singly definitive, you are more likely to arrive at a valid indication of the qualities you're seeking.

So let's add some additional methods to assess the biker candidates. In completing your list of evidence under "Demonstrates by..." you might write, in addition to your obstacle course observations, "candidate responses to interview questions indicate an attitudinal and emotional orientation appropriate to safe riding." What kind of interview question might test for those qualities? "You look like you can really ride that thing! Tell me about the wildest thing you've ever done on a bike!" (Your eager, enthusiastic flattery might trip up a faker.) Answers that would be evidence for (though not proof of) the desired qualities might include, "Wild? Gee. I once rode to the grocery store on a whim," or "Well, I do some awesome dirt biking on the weekends. But I always get my thrills in the woods where the only person I could possibly hurt is me."

You might also probe for maturity and responsibility components (from the ethical capacity). "Can you tell me about a time you made a big mistake, perhaps even completely by accident? And what did you do about that?" Of course, you're looking for someone who takes responsibility by owning up to errors, and looking for signs that they did responsible things in light of their goof.

You now have two bases for assessing competence in the desired capacities. But someone with sufficient guile and brains could still mislead you. That's why you might want to add a third assessment device: testimonials from references attesting to the candidate's responsible nature without indications of tendencies toward immature, irresponsible behavior. "Hello, Mr. Gutierrez. Tim Carter gave me your name as someone who knows him pretty well. Tim's applied for a position with my company and I'm trying to learn a little bit more about him. Would you mind telling me how long you've known him?

Yeah, he seems great! I really enjoyed meeting him. He's a fun-loving guy, isn't he? What's he like when he gets really 'wild 'n' crazy'?"

If there's any doubt in your mind, or you just want to cover all the bases, you could add a fourth assessment device to the list: indications of high-responsibility orientation as assessed by a reliable standardized personality profile instrument (see next chapter).

Defining "what competence looks like" seems to many a little unnatural at first. We make so many inferential leaps in daily life that we rarely have to pull our assumptions apart and dissect how we've reached a judgment. Once you shift into the "prove it" way of thinking, it becomes easier to detail what reasonably constitutes evidence for a given quality. Without question, there are going to be times when you aren't sure if your assessment evidence statements or your means for testing are exactly right. The key to creating usable assessments, according to assessment expert Grant Wiggins, is to meet four simple but powerful criteria: Make sure they are *credible*, *fair*, *honest*, and *useful*. Your assessments may not be perfect, but when your thorough, multiple-method assessment process is complete, they'll probably have done the job much better than if you had not used the process.

TRACKING CANDIDATE ASSESSMENTS

Now that you have your Key Qualifications Profile for all the vital capacities you insist that your new hire have, you'll need to track each candidate's progress as he or she is analyzed by the assessment measures. To do that, use the Candidate Assessment Grid, Figure 6-3.

Let's walk through the Grid. You'll use a different copy of the Grid for each candidate you assess. Recording all key indicators of a candidate's capacity to do the job well—or, as you'll see below, to possibly cause you trouble—simplifies the job of comparing one candidate with another. Naturally, this makes your selection decision considerably easier than trying to keep the

Assessing Applicants: A Process   123

Natural Selection Hiring Method™
Candidate Assessment Grid

Capacity/Behavior	Rating/Type of Capacity or Behavior	Method of Assessment	Evidence/Basis for Judgment	Candidate's Demonstrated Competence Level	Hiring Decision Weight	Notes

Figure 6-3. The Candidate Assessment Grid helps you track all-important evaluative information for a candidate in one consistent, easy-to-complete form.

blur of bodies and names and qualifications and deficiencies and liabilities all straight in your head or scattered about in disparate notes and files.

Capacity/Behavior Column. In the first column, list the capacity or work behavior that you are assessing. Pick up the language for this column from the first column of the same name in the Key Qualifications Profile. Later in the assessment process, you'll likely add capacities and behaviors to the list as your candidate assessments lead you to discover interesting strengths and liabilities in specific applicants, as discussed below.

Rating/Type Column. Enter the criticality rating for this quality from the Job Profile Matrix (Chapter Four). This will be helpful later, when comparing candidates and their various strong points. By refreshing your memory as to how critical the quality is to performing the job well, you'll get a better sense of each candidate's strengths and shortcomings.

Also use this column later in the process to note the significant characteristics you weren't specifically seeking but which revealed themselves through your assessments of the candidate. Your assessments may reveal that an individual has many significant characteristics that could impact your selection decision either positively or negatively. Capture those unexpected qualities by identifying them in the first column, and describe them in this column as either a bonus quality or as an unacceptable/liability characteristic.

A bonus quality is a capacity or work behavior that, while not necessarily required for the job, could be of great value to the organization. Perhaps this could be an "extracurricular" quality, such as serving on a task force. Other examples might include fluency in a foreign language, having an extensive network of contacts in the industry or profession, or achievement in work experience not directly related to the position you're filling but potentially applicable to another post within the organization.

An unacceptable/liability characteristic is when a candidate exhibits behaviors that are inappropriate or offensive, or has attributes which make him unsuitable and unacceptable or which are likely to impair performance. Examples might include strong body odor, unkempt appearance that is inappropriate to executing the duties of the position, inappropriate behavior during assessment (using profanity; making snide, lewd, or threatening remarks to you or your colleagues; having an outburst or being argumentative; and so on), a prohibitive accent, criminal conviction, and so on.

In addition to negative attributes, a candidate may possess attributes that are not negative but are contrary to the nature of the job, or are perhaps even too much of a good thing. Examples of traits that are contrary to the nature of the work might include a clear preference to work alone rather than in a group situation, or vice versa, or a demonstrated preference to work at a slow pace when the job requires speed. Too much of an otherwise desirable capacity can also be a problem. An example of this would be if the candidate were overly cognitive for a position that presents little complexity and requires little or no problem solving. This can lead to boredom or anger, lack of attention to tasks, and other performance shortcomings.

Method of Assessment Column. Enter the source(s) you used to reach the conclusion you did about the candidate's measuring up to (or not) the specific requirements in this column (the capacity/behavior and the demonstrated competence level). This is where you'd list *personal interview on (date), employment reference consulted on (date), work sample provided by candidate*, and so on.

Evidence/Basis for Judgment Column. Use the following scale to indicate how you arrived at your judgment:
D = Demonstrated
R = Represented
U = Unknown (or not assessed)

A demonstrated basis is one where the candidate exhibited the capacity, or you or another member of the assessment team observed the behavior or saw the applicable license, and so on.

A represented basis is where you are relying on something

other than direct observation or proof. When a candidate reports an experience on a résumé, or tells you in an interview that he or she can do or has done such and such, that is a represented capacity. Whatever you hear from an employment reference is represented. The scores from personality, integrity, and behavioral profile tests are represented.

If you could not determine a candidate's competence for a desired quality, or didn't try, indicate that it is unknown.

Candidate's Demonstrated Competence Level Column. Does the candidate have the necessary degree of competence you specified for the required behaviors? Rate the extent to which he or she does reach your standard for each quality you are assessing for using a simple scale.

- ✔ = Competence present at the level described as sufficient to meet the job requirement.
- + = Competence at a level that exceeds the requirement to do the job.
- − = Competence not present.
- −/+ = Developmental. Competence is not at the required level; however, assessments indicate candidate likely could develop sufficient competence.
- ? = Competence unknown, untested, or not demonstrated.

Scoring a capacity as developmental is a tricky judgment call. Using this rating is most appropriate for a deficiency in required technical knowledge or skills. A gap in the technical capacity can be closed with training, mentoring, and experience. Closing gaps in other capacities is arguably much more difficult and carries a greater risk that the worker will never reach competence, and your less-than-qualified candidate will become a less-than-qualified incumbent.

Hiring Decision Weight Column. This is where you declare the relative importance of each quality to your hiring decision.
Must have: You would not hire someone without demonstrable competence in this behavior. Because this list likely excludes more people than it includes, it should be short. If someone could succeed in the job without reaching the desired level of

competence in this behavior, it doesn't belong on the must have list. Your selection screening process should focus strongly on must have attributes.

Desirable: Possessing these characteristics would enhance the value someone in this position could deliver to the organization, but you could live without the candidate demonstrating complete competence in this behavior.

Reject: Fatal flaw. Candidates who demonstrate this characteristic are removed from all further consideration. You could define, in advance, some of the characteristics or behaviors that would trigger an automatic rejection (for example, conviction for violent offense, misrepresentation of credentials, and so on), or decide to apply it later to the behaviors you uncovered during your assessments and entered as unacceptable/liability in the Rating/Type column.

Judgment as Group Activity

Don't assess a candidate using only a single measurement method and don't do it as a solo sport. No matter how conscientious you are, how carefully you monitor your own biases, you'll probably still overlook or misread something. Have colleagues who have also been briefed on sound assessment principles examine your leading candidates. Those evaluators may include the potential hire's prospective peers, bosses, even direct reports and customers. This multi-layered assessment approach is becoming increasingly popular in companies of all sizes and in all industries. There's a good reason for this: The more you have at stake in making a good hire, the more you should want to have a thorough, diverse, and well-rounded assessment.

Compare notes. Look for what psychologists call inter-rater agreement. In other words, examine your assessment conclusions. Where did your analysis and that of your colleague line up and where did they diverge? Do the differences center on the same items (for example, different ratings for critical behaviors in the interpersonal capacity), or is there disagreement about emphasis (for example, some evaluators are emphasizing the relative importance of scores related to one set of capacities while others suggest giving more weight to another set). How can you reconcile the differences in perspective? If there are significant inconsistencies in how members of your evaluation team scored a candidate in a particular performance area, perhaps you should call the candidate back in and clarify some things that may have been misunderstood, or determine if the candidate perhaps was simply inconsistent during the assessments.

SCORING: MANY ARE CALLED, FEW ARE CHOSEN

To determine whether the candidate has the competence you declared as critical to fulfilling the objectives of the job, simply look at the two columns to the left of the Notes column. Highlight each *must have*, then look to the left of each. Is there a check or a plus there? If there are any minus signs, can you still seriously consider this candidate?

> You need a strong team, because a mediocre team gives mediocre results, no matter how well managed it is.
>
> —Bill Gates, CEO, Microsoft

If a candidate lacks competence in the qualities you specified as *must have* to do the job, think hard before extending an offer. Do not hire this person without a specific plan to eliminate such deficiencies. To do so would only condemn the new hire to failure, cheating both the individual and your organization.

The more *desirable* competencies a candidate demonstrates in addition to the *must have* ones, the more likely that person is to do well in a given position, and the greater the potential for adding value beyond the job description.

What *bonus* competencies did you determine that the candidate was bringing with him or her? Might those add value, increase the likelihood of effective cross training, or present transfer or promotion possibilities?

Look at the *unacceptable/liabilities* list you've compiled. Are you prepared to pay this price? Will the benefit be worth the pain over the long haul? Might it be less painful to extend your search?

Remember that there's a difference between hiring the candidate you set out to hire and settling for the "least worst" you've assessed so far. In education, it's called standards versus norming—standards are fixed; judging against normative measures (grading on a curve) is relative. When you move from standards to relative measures, you're usually heading in the wrong direction—away from achieving your outcomes.

That said, your odds of finding someone who is the perfect fit are about the same as playing the state lottery. So inevitably, you'll wrestle with tradeoffs. One way of reconciling the give-and-take between your needs and the candidate pool is suggested by business consultant Bill Lee, who conducts "Hire Your Way to Higher Productivity" seminars throughout North America. He suggests that the final hiring decision involves three factors: applicants' talent (or capacity) to do the job, their experience in doing something similar, and their "chemistry" in fitting with the company culture. The highest odds of success, of course, come with all three factors. But for the second-highest odds, Lee asks, "Which would you sacrifice: talent, experience, or chemistry?" He suggests you give up experience. "After all, you can teach a person; talent and chemistry are pretty much innate."

If you can't find a candidate who meets a sufficient number of the standards you set, go back to the well (there are ideas for doing this in Chapter 10), reexamine the job (is it unreasonably configured? does it pay too little for the caliber of person you're trying to attract?), or reexamine your standards. Are they tied to the real job or do they reflect an unrealistic inflation of qualification? You may find the map in Figure 6-4

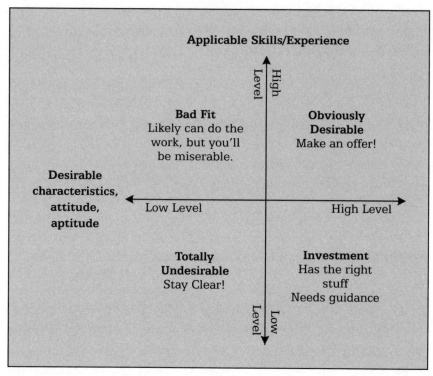

Figure 6-4. In reconciling your assessment of your candidate pool, plotting relative values for technical skills and experience and desirable personal characteristics can give you a "map" to making a decision about whom to hire.

helpful in reconciling your assessments of various candidates.

Finally, remember: the more realistic you are in completing all aspects of the Natural Selection Hiring Method, the more likely you are to hire someone best suited to doing the job well.

Chapter Seven

This Is a Test... This Is *Only* a Test

Select the one statement that most closely reflects your viewpoint: A. I'm always willing to disrupt in order to get what I want done. B. I always rush in getting from one appointment to the other. C. I'm not entirely comfortable walking by a graveyard on a lonely night.

–Caliper Profile
Assessment Instrument Excerpt

Ask business managers for their opinions on employment screening instruments (tests), and you're likely to get strong opinions both favoring and condemning them. Some managers swear they make no impact on hiring other than to drive up selection costs. Others swear the tests make all the difference in the world.

Sears, one of the oldest, most successful American retailers, uses pre-employment screening. Writing in the American Management Association's *Organizational Dynamics*, Peter Cappelli of the Wharton School and Anne Crocker-Hefter of Andersen Consulting report that Sears "relies on some of the most sophisticated selection tests in American industry. The company has refined these tests over time to achieve extremely high predictive power."

Some employers use tests to measure specific aptitudes such as mechanical skills or sales abilities, or characteristics such as trustworthiness. Others test for general intelligence, mechanical ability, or job-specific skills in operating certain types of computer software or running a specific piece of machinery.

> Use of valid selection tests substantially increases the average performance level of the resultant workforce and therefore substantially improves productivity.
>
> –Frank L. Schmidt and John E. Hunter

A Few Words from the Test Makers

Here is the case for employment testing as proffered by the test purveyors industry group, the Association of Test Publishers. This trade association represents dozens of testing concerns, including such notables as Wonderlic Personnel Test, Inc., Educational Testing Service (remember your college SAT exam?), Pinkerton Services Group, The Psychological Corporation, Reid Psychological Systems, Scantron Corp., and corporate giants such as Microsoft and Hewlett-Packard.

> Professionally developed tests that are designed by experts and scored and interpreted by properly trained individuals can help even the most experienced and knowledgeable decision-maker to construct a fairer and more accurate picture of an individual. Using other procedures without considering the results of a good test will tend to rule out more qualified people than will a procedure that includes an appropriate test. Testing, when properly used, results in more motivated, productive, and satisfied workers and less friction and dissatisfaction in the work force. Tests have several advantages over traditional interviews and other commonly used employee hiring and placement procedures. Tests are even-handed; they ask the same questions of everyone.

Tests typically require less time than interviews, so they are more efficient in obtaining job-related information. Appropriate tests have been carefully screened to be fair and unbiased and not to ask for improper information. Tests allow the person's answers to be compared with hundreds or even thousands of other people's answers to the same question under the same standard conditions. Finally, the tests are based on research studies that prove the tests' accuracy and effectiveness. No other procedure can make these claims.

As wonderful as these tests sound for solving your assessment challenge, even the test sellers, who do claim validity and reliability for their assessment instruments, don't want you to rely solely on their products to make your judgment:

> Even a battery of tests should not be the sole deciding factor in hiring or promotion. Properly used, tests are only one part of a process that includes other steps such as application forms, personal interviews, supervisor ratings, and background checks. Considered together, the results of these techniques can provide a more comprehensive picture of an individual to better help an employer make the right decision for both the employee and the company.

So, should you join professional sports teams, major manufacturers, and even top-drawer management recruiting firms who rely on tests to hire their own employees, and use tests? That's a judgment call every firm needs to make for itself.

> Some top recruiters said that the portion of their clients that want to test candidates—even for the chief executive's post—has climbed as high as 30 percent, from a tiny minority a decade ago.
> —The New York Times, September 1996

Good tests, suited to their purpose, can give you information about and insights into a candidate that you might not otherwise obtain. If you are using assessment instruments or giving thought to integrating them into your hiring process, it might be helpful to consider the following points.

Be certain a specific assessment instrument is appropriate for employment screening. Some instruments designed for application in clinical psychology have been used in employment screening, and this may not be entirely appropriate. A test may be valid and reliable only for the purpose it was designed for. (Clinically oriented assessment procedures may be appropriate for some jobs. "We do want to know a prospective police officer isn't out of the 'normal' range before handing a gun to the recruit," explains psychology professor James L. Farr of Pennsylvania State University.)

> We are relying much less on personality profile tests. We found that peer interviews are as or more accurate in predicting an applicant's success in doing the job. And tests need to be read, which can discriminate against some minority groups in which there are varying literacy levels.
>
> —Ann Rhoades,
> Executive Vice President,
> Team Services, Promus Hotel Corp.

To assess a candidate as accurately as possible, test only for qualities that are clearly and defensibly relevant to a business purpose specific to the job. Employment law requires that tests be clearly related to a business purpose. ("We'd like to know who we're getting," is an inadequate justification for testing an applicant.) Know the intended purpose of a particular test and use it accordingly. If you're purchasing an instrument for the purpose of revealing the extent of a particular capacity in a candidate, ask test company representatives to confirm, in writing, that their instrument actually gauges that quality.

Assess the credibility of the specific instrument. Who else uses it? What claims are made for its accuracy? What are the real-world results associated with the test? In other words, if the test is supposed to be good at, say, determining an applicant's suitability for a job, what is the basis for that claim? Are turnover rates for new hires lower at companies that use the test?

Critics of assessment devices caution testers to be especially concerned (even downright wary) about the credibility of any instrument that claims to judge a person's inclination to be honest. Some so-called integrity tests look for personality traits associated with a thieving heart—irresponsible, anti-social, or destructive attitudes or behaviors. Other honesty instruments have come under fire because they all but invite a truly dishonest applicant to fake his responses by "telegraphing" what the desired answers are likely to be. "You've taken without permission, for your own use, equipment, supplies, or merchandise of considerable value from your employer. True or false?" One would have to be stupid as well as dishonest to mess up a question like that.

Honesty tests can pose other problems. "There are questions that will ask you for your reaction to hypothetical dishonest situations, and if you are a particularly kindhearted person who isn't sufficiently punitive, you fail," notes Lewis Malby, director of the American Civil Liberties Union workplace rights office. "Mother Teresa would never pass some of these honesty tests," Malby told *The New York Times*.

Still other honesty tests rely on a mechanical device commonly referred to as a polygraph or lie detector. It measures someone's stress level in response to questions as detected in physiological processes such as heartbeat, blood pressure, and respiration. When people lie, the theory goes, their stress level rises and gives them away. While the polygraph industry claims an accuracy of some 70 percent, the U.S. Supreme Court has its doubts. In an eight-to-one decision in 1998, the Justices upheld a military judge's refusal to admit into evidence a defendant's polygraph results. In the Court's majority opinion, Justice Clarence Thomas declared, "There is simply no consensus that polygraph evidence is reliable," and "certain doubts and uncertainties plague even the best polygraph exams" (*U.S. v. Scheffer*).

Confirm that the tests you're considering actually measure the critical capacities that demonstrably relate to specific job performance. A test that accurately assesses how well one perceives spatial relationships might be perfectly justifiable in screening potential draftspeople or construction supervisors.

It probably is wholly irrelevant for screening an accountant in the construction company. If you are assessing for qualities that don't bear directly on doing the job and do not appear on performance evaluations, you are likely wasting your time and money by purchasing and administering unnecessary tests. Furthermore, you risk legal ramifications for potentially unfairly discriminating against members of groups for which the government seeks to provide special protection. Before you test anyone, know what you're trying to find. If you aren't really sure of what you're looking for, results from even the most sophisticated and reliable instrument won't tell you if you've found it in any applicant.

> If high scores on tests do not translate into future productive job performance, then organizations stand to waste their business investment in selection tests and risk legal challenges to their hiring and placement decisions.
> –Personnel Systems & Technologies Corporation Web site

Ascertain that the instruments are accurate predictors of success for a particular job in your firm. As you have read in prior chapters, a job exists in the context of a particular organization with its own peculiar culture. A score for an applicant's interpersonal skills might be rated as "too brash" in one company, too passive in another, and just right in a third. How can you tell how well a particular assessment rating correlates to expected performance in a given job in your company? Test it internally with a sample of your employees.

For a given job, take a group of your top performers and an equal number of your bottom performers. Ask them to participate in a pilot project to assess the value of the instrument to your organization. Do not discuss the groupings or any other aspect of your review. Explain that they are "part of a representative sample." Assure your colleagues that the assessment is not intended to evaluate their performance or chances for promotion, nor to do anything other than determine whether the instrument identifies common traits in your company's employees. Tell your employees that no one else in the company will see their individual assessment report; you are gathering collective group data only. Promise that you will provide the confidential results of their individual assessment to them and make available a knowledgeable resource to explain the assessment instrument and its results.

After the employees complete the assessments and you receive the data, you should be able to see, with the help of the representative from the test company, clear differences between the two groups. If you do not, this specific instrument—even though it may come with impressive and supportable claims of legally sanctioned validity and reliability—may not be valid and reliable for your purpose. Remember this: All reliability and validity data and claims exist in the context of both specific measurements and specific purposes. A bathroom scale certified as valid and reliable to measure weight up to 220 pounds is of dubious value in assessing how much gasoline the service station down the street is holding in its tanks.

Measuring pounds of flesh and gallons of gasoline both involve assessing physical properties, but in different ways for different purposes. The difference is obvious in this crude analogy from the world of physics. Such differences in the less cut-and-dry world of psychometrics are quite often not intuitively obvious.

> Everyone uses some testing system; unfortunately, for most it's called hire and hope.
> –Decision Support Technology Web site

Ask about the test's content validity, its reliability in predicting performance, and how well it satisfies the requirements of the Uniform Guidelines on Employee Selection Procedures. (Those guidelines were adopted by the U. S. Equal Employment Opportunity Commission, the Department of Labor, the Department of Justice, and the Civil Service Commission.) Not all tests or measuring instruments are valid. One needs no license, no approval from any body—governmental or professional—to create and sell assessment instruments. Just because a test asks questions and produces a score or other evaluation information does not mean it accurately measures anything. It may be merely masquerading as a valid instrument, without the underlying research and substance.

So ask a test company about its test's content validity and reliability in predicting specific performance, and its possible adverse impact on minority applicants. If the test company representative, whose business card probably says "consultant," gives you either a blank stare or the slick sales equivalent of "ah, that legal mumbo jumbo and psycho-babble stuff really don't matter none," immediately kick the person out of your office. The instruments he or she represents may or may not be valid and in legal compliance.

But how would you know? And even if they were, what kind of resource to your company do you think that "consultant" would be in helping you through the occasional brambles surrounding employment testing? Some testing consultants may be closer to test peddlers than employment or organizational consultants. Some test companies offer a "certification" to their employees or independent distributors to imply credibility. These declarations of competence may come complete with a set of initials following the person's name. Alphabetic suffixes do not necessarily mean that the test representative has any formal education in psychology, testing methodology, or employment law, or that he or she has passed a state exam, or even has applicable business experience.

Note the prescribed procedures for how the instrument is to be administered and interpreted. Instrument makers may carefully construct a questionnaire designed to reveal the true nature of an applicant. Let's say the designer's explicit instructions are that the instrument is to be completed by individuals working by themselves in one sitting. A careless employer might say to an applicant, "Go ahead and take that thing home and complete it over the weekend." The applicant might then complete the questionnaire in tandem with a roommate, spouse, or group of friends. ("Does this sound like me?" "How do you think they'd want me to answer this one?") That would invalidate the accuracy of the instrument (which is likely pegged at something significantly less than 100 percent anyway).

Use tests appropriately. Herbert Greenberg, president and CEO of the testing company Caliper, says critics of employment testing have some good reasons to snipe at employment tests. There are, he says, many bad tests on the market. And it's no wonder. Any psychologist who's familiar with clinical instruments and wants to break into the corporate market could make inappropriate workplace use of a test designed to discover clinical mental health problems. The tests may not be suitable for determining job-related factors. You don't need to be a psychologist to create an employment-screening test. Anyone can craft and sell a test; you can easily find promotions for homebrew tests with dubious claims for validity on the Internet.

Even well researched and valid employment tests can be misused, Greenberg says. Many companies do bad things with good tests. They can overuse tests, forcing applicants to complete an unnecessary barrage of tests that yield either irrelevant information or a relatively small amount of new information about the candidates. Or they pay too much attention to test scores and make them *the* assessment rather than part of the assessment process. Conversely, some managers pay too little attention to—or outright ignore—test results, hiring candidates they personally like rather than heeding red flags raised by the tests.

> Even intelligent business people are more swayed by a good marketing pitch than by a [testing] research program they don't really understand. That's the unfortunate thing. A person with a slick pitch and no real research behind their tests can have a good business.
>
> –John Kamp
> Industrial Psychologist
> in The New York Times

Managers can also confuse "interest inventories" with aptitude. Just because a candidate has an interest in the work of a job doesn't mean he or she can do it. It's like confusing an interest in playing the piano with having an aptitude for music. Likewise, sharing the interests of people who gravitate to a given occupation doesn't make one qualified for it. Interest inventories may have value in career counseling, but as an assessment device for screening applicants for a specific job, they're of no apparent value.

"Good tests can help a company find someone most suited to a job," Greenberg says, "but they do not replace interviews and reference checking. They're only a percentage of the process and decision."

Don't Mess with My Head

An applicant instructed to complete a "personality profile" might demand to know "If I can do the job, why do you need to get into my head?" Some people bristle at the thought of their "personality" being captured, cataloged, and categorized by a simple paper-and-pencil test or its computerized equivalent. Others strenuously object. Such testing, to some, seems to be an invasion of privacy, an insult to one's humanity, and an assault on individuality.

As a hiring manager, recognize that some people resist testing not because they have something to hide, but for other reasons. They may have test anxiety left over from school, or genuinely fear the test won't treat them fairly, or feel that tests dehumanize them. How can a test dehumanize a person? Think of it this way. If the test isn't accurate, it could cost the applicant a great job. If the test is accurate, it may make the subject feel as though his or her privacy has been violated. The person's psyche will have been laid bare, splayed wide open to reveal deeply personal characteristics to perfect strangers, and there will be no opportunity for consent or rebuttal.

Everyone has reason to doubt the efficacy of a psychological test. It's trying to define and measure the most complex thing on the planet, the human mind. Besides, everyone knows that psychology routinely fails at its most basic task—separating the criminally insane from the rest of us. The failures are infamous: the paroled psycho who strikes shortly after being released for being the perfect picture of a well-balanced human being, the wacko who strikes on the way home from his appointment with his shrink, and so on. If all the accumulated psychological wisdom and the best clinical assessments can't predict if Johnny is going to kill his mother, should we really expect anyone to believe that psychological instruments will accurately predict whether Johnny will take direction from his boss?

Remember that test results are not a person; they are only an indicator. Everyone performs differently in the rich, diverse, and pressured environment of the real world—with its real consequences—than they do in the isolated, solitary, and static test taker's world. For some, that sterile test realm feels safe, even comfortable. For others, it is a frightening, lonely, stress-laden hell. As Howard Gardner, the Harvard researcher who popularized the theory of multiple intelligences, puts it, "By focusing on the knowledge that resides within a single mind at a single moment, formal testing may distort, magnify or grossly underestimate the contributions that an individual can make within a larger social setting."

I know that my own best thinking is invariably in response to the stimuli of others' thoughts expressed in the interplay of questioning and sharing of ideas and experiences. I've never encountered a test that I completed by myself in silence that brought my gray cells to life in anything even approaching that invigorating sense of interaction between minds. Without question, I, for one, am always smarter when engaged in the company of others than thinking alone.

> Test results are not perfect. No procedure that assesses people can be. The best decisions come when test results are combined with information from interviews, expert observations, ratings of past work, and so on.
>
> –Association of Test Publishers

You Have the Right to...

Many organizations require applicants to take tests as a condition for consideration for a post. But they provide little or no information to the prospective employee about what the tests are, why they are required, what information they're likely to ask for, and what will be done with the information obtained from the test. The candidate may not see the results from the test and may not ever hear a word about it. How would you like to be examined and treated that way?

Concerns over how people are treated when a prospective employer tells them to fill out a test form have led to the drafting of a test takers' rights statement. A joint task force representing five professional organizations in education and counseling, including the American Psychological Association, created the proposed statement and a corollary set of responsibilities for test takers, "so that tests may be most validly and appropriately used."

Among its provisions, the statement calls for confidentiality of test results and the right to
- be informed prior to testing about the test's purposes, the nature of the test, whether test results will be reported to you, and the planned use of the results;
- know in advance when the test will be administered, when test results will be available, and whether there is a fee for testing services that you are expected to pay;
- have your test administered and your test results interpreted by appropriately trained individuals;
- know if a test is optional and to learn of the consequences of taking or not taking the test; and
- have test results explained promptly after taking the test and in commonly understood terms.

It's a wise practice to completely share the results of your assessments with your candidates. If they are valid, the candidate likely will marvel at—and appreciate—the thoroughness of your efforts and the insights they brought forth. If the assessments are off the mark, your candidate may very well let you know why. You'll both probably learn something, and you may well avoid a lawsuit for unfair hiring practices.

G AND THE SEARCH FOR INTELLIGENT LIFE

Imagine a test that works like this: Anyone who scores high on it can learn to do most any job. The test—extensively researched, valid, and reliable—almost always accurately indicates that high scorers can deliver high-quality job performance. Would you use it in hiring?

In the lingo of casual speech, this seems to be a no-brainer. In a sense, such tests really do exist. They are *general cognitive ability tests* that assess for what we lay folk commonly refer to as intelligence and what psychologists call g (which essentially translates into the mental capacity to process complexity, as in reasoning and problem solving). Extensive research by academics, consultants, and even the U.S. military shows quite convincingly that such valid and reliable tests actually do correlate highly with performance for most jobs in most occupations and industries. Some suggest that cognitive tests are the best single predictor of job performance. Still, deciding to use these apparent panaceas isn't a no-brainer; they stir considerable controversy in hiring. Turns out that those g tests have a couple of problems.

"Over the past ten to fifteen years, the situation has become more clear—measures of cognitive ability are generally a valid predictor of performance," explains James L. Farr, past president of the Society for Industrial and Organizational Psychology. "But they are a two-edged sword," he says, "because they also often have an adverse impact on minorities."

Adverse impact, in the vernacular of employment law, means some minorities, for a host of reasons, tend not to score as highly on the g tests as the majority population. So they appear to be less qualified (see Chapter 2). That effect adversely impacts on the hiring opportunities available to certain minority groups. The net result is that when an employer uses a g test as an all-purpose filter for hiring, bright and capable people pass through to the keeper side of the filter to be sure, but a disproportionate percentage of minority groups don't make the cut based on test scores.

The second problem is not as apparent as the statistical summaries of test takers' scores, but its impact is somewhat related to the first problem. While it may be true that people who score well on the g tests tend to do well in most professional endeavors they choose to pursue, doing well in many jobs may not depend on high g scores. Depending on g scores as the screening device means essentially telling applicants, "If you don't score well on this, you can't be hired to do that." So, people with a high g score might generally do well as firefighters, but does that mean one absolutely needs a high g score to be a great firefighter?

This brings us back to the correlation issue discussed previously. High scores on a given type of instrument—g tests, for example—correlate highly with success in many jobs. Great. One could look at an applicant's high scores on a g test and, if the other capacities necessary to doing the job seem to be there as well, confidently place a bet on the applicant's future success. So far so good. But a trap lies within the simplicity of this apparent hiring solution. Relying on g scores as the filter lets in potentially good performers but it also screens out many others who might do just as well. The price of admission may be unnecessarily restrictive.

Here's another way to think of the problem: Music teachers say that students who do well on stringed instruments such as the violin tend to do well in learning to play other instruments proficiently. So should a conductor hiring for her orchestra require all applicants to prove proficiency on the violin before hiring them to play drums, tubas, or piccolos?

Relying on a general-purpose assessment that reliably screens in good candidates but unnecessarily screens out others is not a good solution to the complexities of assessing job candidates. To do so potentially harms people by denying them an opportunity to do work they are perfectly capable of doing well, and harms employers seeking to fill posts with capable people.

Intelligence at Work

The Wonderlic Personnel Test (WPT), its maker says, measures general intelligence. The company's claims for the test, published on its Web site, give a hint as to why some employers value an intelligence test as a screen for hiring. According to Wonderlic, people who score high on its intelligence test work differently than people who score lower in the following key areas:

- Learning on the job. Higher scores on the WPT indicate an ability to learn from on-the-job experiences and to draw inferences from diverse sources. In contrast, lower scores indicate that important information will not be recognized unless it is clearly presented.
- Understanding instructions on the job. Higher scores on the WPT indicate an ability to interpret instructions with greater understanding, using a broader base of knowledge and experience. In contrast, lower scores indicate that more explicit instructions and close supervision are required.
- Solving problems on the job. Higher scores on the WPT indicate an ability to draw inferences to find effective solutions to problems that may arise on the job, or even find ways to prevent them. In contrast, lower scores indicate difficulty in dealing with unexpected problems.

Testing...Testing...Testing...

Well-designed tests can be very efficient; they yield a great deal of insight in a relatively brief period of time at a modest cost. With improvements in computer technology and statistical methodology, many tests are, arguably, getting more valid and reliable for a wide variety of applications. Perhaps not surprisingly, the testing industry is booming.

Not every observer takes delight in this. "In addition to standardized tests for students, we have such tests for teachers, supervisors, soldiers, and police officers," notes Howard Gardner. "We can draw on short-answer measures for assessing personality, degrees of authoritarianism, and compatibility for dating. The United States is well on the way to becoming a 'complete testing society.' We could encapsulate this attitude thus: If something is important, it is worth testing in this way; if it cannot be so tested, then it probably ought not to be valued."

Test mania isn't strictly an American phenomenon. Clear around the world in New Zealand, personnel psychologists also debate the merits of validating people through multiple choice. Organizational consultant David Winsborough observes, "We also see some manic behavior in the area of test construction. Literally hundreds of new tests are produced every year. In New Zealand I know of eight organizational psychologists or practices actively engaged in competitive test construction (which must equate to a sizable percentage of the nation's organizational psychologists). Likewise the number of versions sometimes produced means they seem to be designed to last for a limited time (finite shelf life). 'Fresh tests' regularly updated have some theoretical appeal, but this is not, we suspect, always driven by a love of test theory or interest in advancing the field."

Winsborough has a solution to companies' apparently increasing dependence on test results for decision making and gullibility to test makers' sometimes-fanciful claims. "We have constructed our own test to measure whether individuals are susceptible to blind acceptance of hyperbole and advertising claims because they think that technical reliability stuff is cushion stuffing. We call it the Reliability? Irrelevant! Didn't I Order a Test? Test (Reliable IDIOTS©)... The scoring is completely user determined (which helps the norms no end)."

TEST MART

Psssssst! Wanna buy some tests?

Here is information about popular employment tests, with contact information for their purveyors.

Wonderlic Personnel Test, Inc. claims that over 100 million people have taken a Wonderlic test in its more than sixty years as an employment test maker. The company markets its flagship Wonderlic Personnel Test as "a short, yet proven accurate measure of general intelligence" that "dramatically reduces employee training time and turnover by helping you match candidates with jobs that complement their mental abilities." The company also markets aptitude tests, basic verbal and numeric skills tests, and technical skills tests developed by the National Occupational Competency Testing Institute (NOCTI).

These "specific tests to assess a candidate's level of mastery of a trade or profession" are said to prevent you from hiring job candidates "who do not possess the specific knowledge required to perform their job." Tests cover a wide range of technical knowledge from accounting and air-cooled gas engine repair to nursing and robotics.

Wonderlic also markets a "behavioral questionnaire" called the Employee Reliability Inventory that the company says "identifies 'low risk' candidates who are likely to perform their job in a reliable manner." The ERI, Wonderlic claims, "assesses the following areas of behavioral risk: freedom from disruptive alcohol and illegal drug use, courtesy, emotional maturity, conscientiousness, trustworthiness, long-term job satisfaction, safe job performance." The company says it also offers "interview and follow-up reference checking questions based on the test results."

Wonderlic also sells its 16PF™ Personality Profile, an assessment often used in selecting managers and executives, and many other instruments, including one that is intended to help employees become more entrepreneurial. It also sells other employment-related products and services. The company is based in Chicago. Contact: (800) 963-7542; Web site: www.wonderlic.com.

Caliper claims to have "the largest body of data in the world relating personality to job performance." The Caliper Profile is "one of the most highly researched instruments in the world in terms of its ability to assess personality" and "has a high degree of predictive validity." The company says its data show that people it has recommended for hiring "produce at a substantially higher level and turn over at a substantially lower level" than people hired against its recommendation.

Caliper says it uses a process of "matching an individual's central strengths to the fundamental requirements of a specific job." It guarantees its work. "If a recommended individual does not work out as described in the test and has to be terminated, we will test that person's replacement free of charge." The company has served "well over 23,000 corporate clients throughout the world," and has been involved in programs to place more than 3,500 previously "hard core" unemployed individuals into "a wide range of productive jobs." Caliper also offers services for testing "the inner athlete" for professional sports firms. It is headquartered in Princeton, NJ. Contact: (609) 924-3800; e-mail: writeus@caliperonline.com; Web site: www.caliperonline.com.

Reid Psychological Systems, makers of employment tests for more than fifty years, sell tests purported to identify trustworthiness, previous criminal behavior, previous drug abuse, and attitudes about safety; also, the company makes tests for customer service skills, numerical skills, sales productivity, management potential, and more. Reid is based in Chicago. Contact: (800) 922-7343; Web site: www.reidsystems.com.

Consulting Psychologists Press, Inc. is the publisher of the ubiquitous *Myers-Briggs Type Indicator (MBTI)*, which its maker describes as an "inventory" that is "the most widely-used personality inventory in history," with some two-and-a-half million people having taken it in a year. Unlike many of their test-making brethren, CPP declares that certain tests published by them are only available to "users who have appropriate training and credentials, and who adhere to the principals of proper test use, including knowledge of tests and their use." To administer the MBTI, an authorized licensee "must have a degree from an accredited college or university and have satisfactorily completed a course in the interpretation of psychological tests and measurement at an accredited college or university."

CPP also markets the California Psychological Inventory, which "provides an accurate, complex portrait of a client's professional and personal style" that the company says is useful for employee selection, developing leadership and teamwork skills, and so on. CPP is located in Palo Alto, CA. Contact: (800) 624-1765 or 650/969-8901; e-mail: custserv@cpp-db.com; Web site: www.cpp-db.com.

VALIDITY AND CORRELATION: FREUDIAN SLIPS?

If you go shopping for employment tests, you'll hear various claims about reliability and validity. Reliability relates to the consistency of test results. Validity is a bit more complex. Test validity is expressed as a correlation—the relationship between this factor and that variable, between a measurement on a test and the rate greater than merely by chance at which it correlates to the factor being measured. Do you find yourself a little foggy on this whole concept so central to test validity? Most people are.

Correlation expresses the linear relationship between two variables (this and that). For example, let's say you are testing the relationship between pressing the doorbell button on your front door (this) and the number of times the doorbell actually rings (that). You press the button twenty times and the bell rings twenty times. That is a 1:1 relationship, a perfect correlation, which can be expressed as 1.0. That gives a strong hint of causality between pressing the button and the bell ringing but does not establish it absolutely. A correlation of zero implies no relationship at all; this would be the case if no matter how many times you pressed the button, the bell rang no more than it would at random.

Interestingly, a "valid" correlation between a this and a that is not necessarily anywhere close to a one-to-one relationship. A positive correlation between two factors suggests that when this increases, that also increases to some degree. When two factors have a high correlation (the nearer to 1.0, the stronger the correlation), the stronger the implication that they are related. (The classic joke about correlation suggests that trailer parks cause tornadoes. That's because of the apparently strong correlation between damage in trailer parks—"mobile home communities," as they are called now—and tornado sightings.) Most variables studied for correlation do not correlate at the 1.0 level (including the pressing of the button on my front door and the chiming of the doorbell in my home).

In assessment, a correlation might be established between an instrument's or procedure's measurement (score) and the actual occurrence—or not—of the thing being measured. For example, let's say we're going to use your aunt Polly's occasional leg pain as a test for whether it's going to rain (she swears by it). We keep accurate data of every time Auntie reports that her knee is "acting up again" (this). We also keep years of detailed meteorological data on when it rains outside Auntie's house (that). We correlate Aunt Polly's pain reports with rainfall to determine if her aching knee is a valid assessment device for predicting rain. If every time she complains about pain, the sun shines for the next two days, there would be a perfect negative correlation (or -1.0) between her pain and rain. But if your data show that her complaining precedes the rain more often than it would by chance, you might have a valid weather forecaster in the family. If that correlation were at the 0.1 level, you might not consider it so valid that you would depend on it. But if it were .65, would you head out to a picnic before calling dear old Auntie?

Of course, industrial and organizational psychologists study relationships more complex and less discernible than the one between your button and doorbell, or Polly's pain and precipitation. They may conduct studies to correlate, for example, people's optimism (defined by a great number of thises and thats) with their absentee rates. Or they may watch the way one tends to faux tasks stacked up in a simulated in-box (dispatching many thises and thats) while being observed, and then correlate their evaluation of the performance in the simulation with evaluations of the actual effectiveness of an executive performing in the real world.

So, not surprisingly, most studies by psychologists don't show a correlation between two variables at anywhere near a 1.0 level. A correlation of, say, .75 is considered high, and it's rare. Many published studies that hypothesized a strong correlation between this and that—whatever they may be—show a positive correlation of less than .33.

In measuring the correlation between the thises and the thats, massive amounts of data can be gathered and analyzed (and, more recently, meta-analyzed, which involves the large-scale re-analysis of analyses). Much of what appears to be scientific "proof" of a given study's findings or of a particular instrument's validity is a mountain of statistics manipulated and massaged using every imaginable mathematical model and statistical technique. The resulting tables—cross-referenced and analyzed in infinite configurations with numeric gymnastics—appear to be most sophisticated, and, therefore, accurate and precise. Yet, despite volumes of studies and analyses gathered over decades, nothing in organizational psychology is ever definitive. It cannot be so, and that is fundamental.

In measuring the relationship between this and that, the variables often are people—who are notoriously unpredictable and inconsistent with one another. So the variables are never precisely the same in any two studies, and may not be the same in any two people in any one study (or even the same in the same person, on some days). Furthermore, unlike physical scientists who can isolate the subjects of their studies in a controlled environment, organizational psychologists can never truly isolate this and that from the myriad study-polluting influences of the terribly messy world in which we all operate. So every organizational psychology study—or instrument or conclusion that grows from it—faces two insurmountable challenges in definitively stating that this relates indisputably to that: namely, this and that themselves and the world at large.

Precision is impossible. All psychological measurements are inaccurate; some are more so than others. Validity is a relative term, and it is awfully far from certainty.

The most valid way to use a test is as an indicator among several others. The more complete your assessment process (using a variety of assessment methods), the more valid your conclusions about a candidate are likely to be. Even the test companies say that.

Chapter Eight

Interviewing: "So, Tell Me About Myself"

> Most people hire people they like, rather than the most competent person. Research shows that most decision-makers make their hiring decisions in the first five minutes of an interview and spend the rest of the interview rationalizing their choice.
>
> –Orv Owens, Psychologist
> in The New York Times

Interviewing—talking with and getting to know someone—is, for some managers, about as natural an act as any in management. For others, it may represent one of the most dreaded, intimidating, and stressful (almost as stressful as *firing* someone) managerial obligations. Still others see it as a chance for a little diversion from the routine, an opportunity to pull out those "killer" questions and maybe dish out some intimidation—not for the fun of it, of course, but to see how the candidate handles "the rough and tumble of the real world." For many others, it's just another task in a long day; grab and skim the résumé or employment application as the applicant is taking a seat, and start firing the old standby questions.

Regardless of their orientation to interviewing, for most managers this crucial responsibility represents both a large investment of time and a tedious exercise that they approach without considerable forethought or regard for how they do it.

No matter how you feel about interviewing, chances are good that you have approached it with less than a rigorous structure and reliable methodology. If you are among those few who do use a consistent approach to your candidate interviews, this chapter may challenge some of your assumptions (for example, what's wrong with interview questions focused on behavioral anecdotes). The Natural Selection Hiring Method brings structure and methodology to this crucial aspect of candidate assessment and hiring.

FOR SALE: APPLICANT, MINT CONDITION; READY, WILLING, AND ABLE

By the time you sit across the desk from a candidate, you're deep into the process we've outlined in this book, so you already know a great deal of what you're looking for and should know a great deal about the candidate already. But your job is to find out who that person really is, to see through the job hunter's carefully crafted campaign to communicate, "buy *me.*" Your inquiries must cut through the candidate's trimmed, polished, and coiffed *Monday-go-to-interview* veneer.

Job applicants have at their disposal literally shelf after shelf of books in any bookstore telling them how to construct the perfect résumé and how to tell you, in a most convincing way, exactly what you want to hear during the employment interview. Many applicants have been coached, videotaped, and rehearsed by professional job counselors. They know all the standard answers, and they've practiced snappy retorts to even the toughest standard questions. In short, many job applicants are much more skilled and much better prepared for their side of the interview than the person sitting across the desk from them (who, frankly, may not be prepared or skilled at all).

Many interviews unfold as a battle, not of wits but of *sales pitches*. The candidate is selling the best employee anyone ever heard of, with the hiring manager pitching feverishly, "what an absolutely fantastic opportunity this job is even though you can't tell from the salary." Rather than play dueling advertisements, the hiring manager needs to be a careful buyer and skilled interviewer to cut past the candidate's commercial.

> Because job applicants are becoming increasingly sophisticated, it is not unusual for a company to inadvertently hire an individual who makes the best impression, rather than the person who is best suited for the position.
>
> –User's Guide, Caliper

This chapter provides you with a structure and a method to greatly improve the quality of information and insight that you can extract from a prospective hire during a carefully planned and executed job interview.

CAN YOU RECALL A TIME WHEN YOU ASKED A QUESTION?

An interview technique that's been around for decades has become quite fashionable recently. Known by many names, most of which have the term *behavior* in them, this technique is predicated on a simple premise: A look at the past provides a glimpse of the future; if you did it before, you'll do it again. The basic script calls for the interviewer to prompt, probe, or press the candidate to recall and describe in sometimes excruciating detail a real-life incident that provides evidence of a skill or experience relevant to the new job. The fundamental precept is that there is a world of difference between talking a good game, being there when it is played, and actually carrying the ball.

Behavior interviews seek evidence that a candidate actually has behaved in the way he or she represents. Rather than listening to an applicant espouse love for teamwork, the interviewer asks, "When was a time when you made a significant contribution to a team and didn't get credit for it?" Instead of letting a candidate assert that she has "strong organizational skills," the interviewer asks, "How did you organize your week last week? Walk me through the planning and organizing process step by step, in as fine detail as you can." When an interviewee asserts that he's a "people person," the interviewer tests that claim by asking, "Can you give me an example of a time when you had a conflict with a coworker over something that was job-related?" If the applicant can't think of a single disagreement, he couldn't possibly be a people person; he's not interacting with anyone.

Entire books have been filled with little more than sample questions for eliciting behavioral descriptions relating to a variety of occupations and situations. But the principle is fundamentally simple and can be illustrated without requiring a book full of examples.

Here's the basic format. The question/imperative urges the candidate to *give a specific example* in a *real instance* of his or her *own action* that *illustrates* and *suggests* competence in a *particular quality*. For example, if you want to test for a customer-focused work orientation (from the practical capacity in the Performance Processes Domain), you could ask, "Could you recall a time when, on your own initiative, you stopped work in progress because you thought it was unacceptable to your customer? What was the circumstance?" And after hearing about the incident, "How did you know what would be acceptable to a customer? Weren't you concerned you might get in trouble for having to start over again?"

If you wanted to assess the candidate's emotional maturity in the workplace, you might ask, "Can you tell me about a recent time when you had to deal with a person who was nasty with you or who made you angry?" You get to the quality by asking for a situation when it should have been present. This is, essentially, the opposite of the exercise you did to profile the job, where you went from task to personal capacity. Here, hoping to find that the candidate actually behaved in a way that would exemplify the capacity, you ask for a situation in which it could have been manifested.

The sample question above opens more avenues than flatly asking, "Have you ever blown up in anger at a coworker or customer?" If the candidate gives you a flat no, you've learned nothing; and a yes might be dismissed with, "Oh, that was so long ago and we're such good friends now. She must have been having a bad day that day." Sure, you could explore this a little more. You might have detected the blaming of the colleague. You could use the behavior-specific approach in probing for more details only if you got a yes rather than a flat no, which would leave you with no information and no applicable insight into the candidate.

If you understand the principles behind the examples above, and can grasp how the following preambles fit with similar interrogatories, you pretty much have the concept down.

- When was a time when you...?
- Can you give me an example of when you...?
- Could you tell me about a time when you...?
- Tell me more about when you...
- Have you ever had to...? What was the situation, and what did you do?
- Describe a situation where you...
- Let's go back to that situation you just mentioned. Can you elaborate a little more about how you...?
- When [this] happens, what do you do? Can you explain in detail a specific instance of that?
- Your résumé/application indicates that you... How exactly did you do that?
- I hear what you're saying, but I need a few more details to really understand what happened. Can you take me back to the point when you...?
- You said that you always/never... But what about a time when...?
- Have you ever had the experience of... (or occasion to...)? Can you tell me about that?

- This is a most impressive accomplishment. To help me understand it better, could you walk me through the process starting with...
- Interesting. Fascinating. Hmmm. No kidding? Wow. Tell me more.
- Cutting expenses 94 percent while increasing revenues 212 percent is most impressive. How did you do that?
- I see. [Silence.] Go on.
- I'm a little confused about what exactly you did in that situation. Can you help me to understand by describing it the way you would describe a scene in a movie, so that I can see the action taking place?
- What were you doing while all this was happening?
- What was your role in that?
- Walk me through, in such fine detail that you think it might annoy me, a typical operation/job/phone call/meeting...
- Recall a time when you grasped the concept and didn't need any more examples.

Similar to past-behavior interview questions are so-called *scenario* questions. This is where you present a situation and ask, "What would you do?" This form of question can be a useful gauge of a candidate's knowledge of a subject or understanding of an ideal response. The candidate's answer doesn't necessarily have any predictive validity in indicating the likelihood that they would actually follow their own script. You might be getting the business equivalent of a well-crafted fairy tale. Follow it up with this question: "What's a similar example from your own life?"

Bear this simple truth in mind when spinning out scenario questions: **Hypothetical questions generate hypothetical answers.**

BEYOND BEHAVIORAL AND SCENARIO INTERVIEWS

Now, there's nothing wrong, per se, with asking for and hearing out some of the candidate's actual experiences. You'll hear loud echoes of that concept here. The fact is that the well-executed past-behavior-based interview is a light-year from where most hiring interviews were in effectiveness just a few short years back. The new dimension here is to recognize the liabilities and limitations of past-behavior-oriented interviews as they are typically executed, and to add some enriching strategies to give you a deeper insight than a superficial tour, punctuated by excruciating detail, through someone's career and life scrapbook.

So let's address the question we've asked: How can listening to what a candidate has really *done*—as opposed to the outcome of the old, informal interview where you listened to what candidates *say* they believe or what they *think* you want to hear—be bad? In truth it may not be, *if* you're sure you want to...

- repeat the past;
- believe an anecdote reveals a pattern;
- really drill down into the specifics even when it's difficult and uncomfortable to do so;
- effectively deduce how representative the candidate's example is, what motivated it, and the likelihood that this is the candidate's instinctual or habitual way of handling similar situations now and forever; and
- tie the string of anecdotes into clearly revealing the many non-technical capacities you're seeking in the candidate;

And if you're sure you know why the candidate did what she did in the stories she told you, and you know what those anecdotes told *her*; and if you're sure the candidate *wanted* to behave this way, and would do so again in similar circumstances but in a different organizational environment, then this is the clincher.

That new environment, yours for example, may offer the candidate different choices because it has its own rules, policies, incentive programs, managerial oversight or support, and so on.

Many managers, practicing a surface-level, give-me-an-example, past-behavior interview, fail these *if* tests. Furthermore, while "behavior-based interviews are great for revealing some past behavior," according to Herb Greenberg of Caliper, the large international employment testing and consulting firm, "it benefits those with applicable experience, people who know the industry or know the lingo." In other words, managers hear familiar terms and references to scenarios they recognize and their judgment about a candidate begins to suffer from what psychologists call the *halo effect*. That's where you confer on your candidate positive points that he may not deserve because his apparently-closely-related-to-yours experience has you identifying with him and convincing yourself that he sounds exactly right for the job.

Hearing familiar buzzwords and instantly recognizable on-the-job situations prompts managers to fill in the gaps in the candidate's story with their own narrative. Because they know (or they *think* they know) where the story is headed, they may actually cut off the candidate prematurely. They clip the reply before really understanding the candidate's precise role in the situation, why she did what she did, exactly how, what the consequences were, whether this was a one-time event, or to what extent this is indicative of the way this candidate usually operates, or wants to operate, and so on. Candidates with closely related prior experience can, even unwittingly, tell the hiring manager exactly what he or she was hoping to hear, so much so that the manager doesn't even need to hear but a fraction of it before leaping to a set of conclusions that may or may not be correct.

When you probe for what a candidate has done behaviorally, particularly when assessing technical experience, be sure to get a sense of *scope* for the behaviors a candidate describes. Just as you profiled the job in terms of criticality, duration, and frequency, you need to get a sense of the same for what candidates say they do. *Example:* the candidate describes working with people, or as part of a team. Probe: *How often? For how long? How important is that to accomplishing the job? Is it your sense that this is too much or too little?* Without a sense of scope, you hear about an isolated incident with no context and no predictive validity.

Can Do vs. Want to Do

Using a software program called Smart Hire® that automatically generates some past-behavior questions that match the general nature of a job, I interviewed someone for an open position in my office. The young man deftly recalled relevant incidents from his experience, some of which were exactly on-point with the requirements for the business card scanning technician post. I was amazed by how well this applicant's interview responses and applicable past experience matched the entire lineup of high-quality questions clearly and appropriately geared to identifying a good match for the job. The questions got at just the right qualities and this candidate could not have had a more perfect set of answers to the very specific questions.

I was all set to hire this perfect match. Then it dawned on me. I could not rely on that series of questions and near perfect answers. Despite all indications to the contrary, I knew the applicant wouldn't work out in the post. Absolutely not, no way! I had been misled.

That candidate was my teenage son, who had already done business card scanning and other administrative chores in my office. He had faithfully performed every function and engaged in every behavior that he truthfully relayed to me during our interview. But he hated the work! Still, he could easily regale me with tales of the detailed and organizational work he had performed. But he did so without betraying one shred of the tedium, disgust, and resentment he felt while doing it, because nothing in the script prompted that. The matter-of-fact questions elicited matter-of-fact answers. All true but far from the whole truth.

We laughed ourselves silly after we both recognized what had happened, but we did the interview absolutely straight. I asked the computer-generated questions verbatim, he answered them as though he were really interviewing for the post. I swear, if I did not know the little silver-tongued slickster, he would have fooled his old man.

I absolutely and most confidently would have hired the kid, on the spot, convinced that I had made one of the best placements of my career. And just as certainly, I would have lost that "perfect" employee in short order. Aaron does not care for detail work. Though his work ethic and commitment to quality are high, the longest he can focus on a repetitive, tedious task like scanning business cards is about an hour a day. Nothing in the "tell me about a time when..." questions even hinted at the problem.

My young applicant could look me straight in the eye, tell me absolutely relevant stories of having performed the work, and could say confidently, "I can do this." But nothing in the behavior-only approach got even close to asking, "Do you *want* to do this work?"

The challenge in interviewing, says Terri Kabachnick, of the successful management consultancy bearing her name, is to get past litanies of prior experiences to understand a job candidate's *core values and beliefs*. "Past behavior does not indicate future performance," warns Kabachnick. "Successful people can fail; fired people can perform."

Even the origin of the word *behavior* speaks to this. It comes from a French root meaning *to have*, as in to *have done before*—not *will do again and again*. There are better indicators of future performance than snapshots of past performance to those who are prepared to read the signs. This involves uncovering applicants' beliefs about autonomy on the job; their feelings about their own self-importance; attitudes about working with other people; orientation toward service; the relative motivational impact of factors such as power, knowledge, and money; and so on. Past-behavior interviewing as typically conducted does little or nothing to unveil these more fundamental and more powerful drivers of your candidate's future behavior, which will potentially be at work in your company's work environment.

Interviewing: "So, Tell Me About Myself"

Your firm may produce a similar product in the same or a similar industry to the one(s) in which your candidate has prior experience. But your culture, your management style, and your expectations for many aspects of job performance may be radically different than the ones where the candidate engaged in behaviors that sound so close to what you're looking for. Or, if they were similar, knowing *how* candidates went through the motions of the behavior they describe doesn't tell you by itself if they liked doing that, if such behavior would be their preference, if they are truly productive while engaged in such behavior, and so on. Perhaps they're replaying their one story of a behavior you asked to hear about, or they are now playing back, like a tape recorder, old war stories of how they went through a set of motions, like a machine, because that's what another employer wanted from them. You learn what they *did*, but not what they *would* do.

In essence, the candidate can tell you a good story, one you want to hear, but one he might not ever want to experience again—unless he had to for money.

> Managers in high-tech, bio-tech, and other engineering-driven fields tend to interview around technical assessment of ability. But their management time isn't spent there! They should focus more on whether the candidate will be happy and successful in their company culture. Is the fit one where it's conducive to the employee's being productive and pleasant?
>
> –Alan D. Davidson
> Psychologist and Hiring Consultant

VALUES AT WORK

The quality of a person's performance on the job will be driven by a number of factors. High among such factors is the individual's unique personal values—what they consider important or worthwhile. Value judgments color a person's life and work-related priorities and choices. Values with motivating power come in many flavors. They include:

- social acceptance (prestige, respect by superiors, peers, colleagues);
- health and safety for oneself or others;

- serving, social responsibility, and the need for doing good;
- ethics and doing the right thing;
- power, influence, and responsibility;
- money and material comfort;
- working environment (inside/outside, comfort, aesthetics);
- adventure and risk;
- certainty (tested and proven tradition);
- challenge;
- trendiness;
- degree of fun;
- learning, discovery, and variety;
- physical work;
- idea work;
- organizational structure and support; and
- independence and freedom.

The list of capacities in the taxonomy detailed in Chapter 4 describes *what* people do in the workplace and *how* they do it. This list of motivators explains *why* people do what they do. The more clues you detect in the interview by listening closely, the more indication you'll get about someone's true orientation. Candidates may wax eloquent about teamwork and even describe their team participation in minute detail, but you may keep hearing about how "I got that back on track," or how the "discussions were great in getting a lot of ideas on the table, but things dragged until I grabbed the bull by the horns and ..."

> *People take only their needs into consideration, not their abilities.*
> –Napoleon I

What to do when you detect such apparent conflicts or inconsistencies? Put them on the table: "Frank, you obviously have some great team experiences, but am I accurately sensing that you wouldn't mind running your own operation?" I've seen candidates stop in the middle of their stride with a stunned look of recognition and say, "You know, you're right. I hadn't really thought seriously about that," or "I didn't think I could find an opportunity to do that."

Certainly, Frank could deny the conclusion you drew. Watch the body language. Listen for the tone of the interview to change. Frank will reveal himself. Give him the chance. Probe for motivation as well as behavior. *Why did you do it that way? What was the drawback to that approach?* That last question, and variations on its negative theme, get the candidate focused on the negative aspects of a method or policy. You give the applicant permission—an excuse—to wedge open the door a crack, and the pent-up, held-back emotions may push it wide open. You'll see either the real Frank, or an extremely controlled actor. (If he's that good, he may well pull it off day-to-day on the job. Still, as the Japanese proverb suggests, sooner or later you act out what you really think.)

VALUING APPLICANTS

The values component comes through when you go beyond behaviors or hypotheticals and probe deeper. When the applicant finishes the anecdote exemplifying the behavior, follow up with questions that get at how the person *felt* about doing that.

- Why did you do it that way?
- What surprised you about the result?
- What kind of an experience was that for you personally?
- On a scale of one to ten, with one being *awful* and ten being *fantastic*, how would you rate that experience for you personally?
- Given your perspective, is that the way you prefer to work? Why?
- Did you receive adequate credit for your efforts?
- Why do you think the situation was approached in that way?
- What was the most difficult part of that for you? Why?
- What did you think of that? Did that make sense to you?
- Should that have been done differently?
- Was that your preference? How would you *like* to have seen it done differently? If it was your call to make, how would you have decided? Why?

- What was wrong with that approach?
- If you had your preference, how would you...?
- How did that decision strike you?
- What was your biggest frustration with...?
- If you could do that over again, how would you approach it?

Why are values so important when you really are hiring someone to go through a set of motions and execute definable, describable, and flowchartable behaviors? For the same reason "value statements" became popular for companies to declare for themselves. Because values guide decisions and actions. The pace of business moves too fast to get permission or consult the policy manual. People will, by necessity, have to act on instincts that are guided by their personal values. Past behaviors help to indicate a pattern of what people *have done*; values indicate the pattern of what people *will do*.

> You're already using psychology—every time you try to guess a motive, figure out a tactful response in a difficult situation, or find a way to explain something effectively.
> –William Bridges
> Author and Consultant

So do you need to be a psychologist to interview effectively? No. You need an interview plan (see below), and very focused listening. If you don't listen closely, you'll miss the clues to the real person whom your questions will reveal if only you'll listen to the answers.

Here are some questions that ask directly for value answers. As with any interview question, candidates can give you answers they think you want to hear. So watch for what test makers call "internal validity"; that's where you hear consistent themes in different answers to different questions. Keep notes. Quote the candidate directly. At some point, ask the real candidate to "stand up"—consistent with his or her pre-interview promise (see below) to not feed you "desirable" answers to the questions you ask.

- What was your position called? Was that an appropriate name for it? (This potentially indicates need for prestige.)

- What was your favorite part of that job?
- If you could redesign that work, how would you? Why?
- When was the last time you broke the rules to get the job done?
- Did you use a dugleflurp to do that? (Use a made-up word. People with self-confidence and commitment to quality will say they don't know what it means.)
- Given a choice between more money or more time for your own interests, which would you choose? (Can use with any two values in the list.)
- What's the most fun you ever had while working?
- What joy do you get or have you gotten from working?
- Have you had the experience where you poured your heart and soul into a project that was then scrapped? What happened? What did you do?
- What's the most foolish thing you've done while on the job? (Does the person have the self-confidence to fess up? Can he laugh at himself? Did she learn from the experience?)
- Sometimes things move pretty fast. Have you ever needed to "make it up as you went along"? Did you check with your boss? How did you feel about that?
- What's something that you did at work that maybe no one else knows about but you are very proud of?
- What's an example of your going "above and beyond the call of duty"? Why did you do it? What regrets do you have about doing it?
- What's the most frustrating part of your current (or last) job?
- Sometimes things get a bit crazed around here. If I asked you to lie for me, would you? (Marketing consultant Richard Weylman says, "If you'll lie *for* me, you'll lie *to* me.")
- Let's say you took this job, and two weeks into it you knew you had made a mistake and wanted to leave. What would make you want to do that?
- Did you receive feedback on your job performance at your last position? How often? Was that often enough? Was it helpful? Why? What were some areas of development in your last feedback session? What did you think of that?

- How would this job fit in with your long-range plans?
- What's a job you've had that wasn't very satisfying?
- What was the "best mistake" you ever made on the job?
- Every person has a full range of emotions. What's something that really "pushes your buttons," that makes you so angry in an instant that you're ready to blow?
- What's the biggest challenge you faced working in a team environment?
- Under what conditions do you do your very best work?
- What can your boss do to help you deliver your very best work?
- When was a time that you were *prevented* from doing the best job you could, completing a project, or delivering the level of quality you expected to?
- When was the last time you asked for help?
- In your last job, how did the company let you down?
- What's an example of when your employer took unfair advantage of you? What did you do about that?
- Tell me about a coworker you thought the company should have fired but didn't.
- What's the one thing your current job doesn't have that you wish it did?
- What's the one thing your current job has that you wish it did not?
- What's a kind of work you would enjoy doing so much you would do it for free if you could?
- What's a work environment that you would be really uncomfortable in? (Seek both physical and cultural answers.)
- How do you like to be complimented?
- What's the best work-related compliment you ever received?
- When was a time you were thrown some work assignment or responsibility that you really weren't prepared for?

There's far too much emphasis in popular employment literature on the perfect power question from the interviewer, and not much on interpreting the answer from the applicant. When you're listening to the answers to these and other interview questions, stay true to your promise to the applicant that there is no right or wrong answer (see below). Reserve judgment. Just focus on what the candidate is saying to you. Ask clarifying questions. Be sure you understand what the candidate means. Record those key words that tie to the values and capacities lists. Sort them out, circle them, and rank them *immediately* after the interview ends. With an open mind and good notes, you don't need to work hard at interpreting the answers. The relevant themes will come through clearly in the candidate's own words.

> *Those who honestly mean to be true contradict themselves more rarely than those who try to be consistent.*
> –Oliver Wendell Holmes, Jr.
> Justice, U.S. Supreme Court

Life-Long Learning

The workers that you hire today will need to do tomorrow's work. There's no way, from a technical task standpoint, that you can define what exactly that work will look like. So you need to have people in the company who can learn, adapt, and evolve. Hiring people because they executed yesterday's tasks in a way that sounds like it might fit with today's tasks does little to inform you of how well they'll dispatch tomorrow's tasks. You need to find candidates with the learning value, or be willing to turn out today's hires every time the work changes tomorrow.

Review the candidate's background. Does it indicate an orientation toward learning? If it lists recent coursework, training programs, or seminars, find out why the candidate enrolled and who paid for it. Ask, "What's a skill or area of development that you plan to improve? What's your plan for doing it?"

Many of the values questions imply a potential learning experience. But you can zero in on the learning component by asking, frequently if not within every experience and anecdotal sequence, questions such as the fol-

lowing:
- "And what did you take away from that?"
- "What impact did that have on you?"
- "Was there a lesson there?" or "How did that change your approach?"
- "Why does that stick out in your mind?"
- "When did you make that mistake again?"
- "What skills or insights did you gain as a result?"
- "What did you do so that wouldn't happen again?"
- "Are you smarter now than you were then? Why?"

Finally, after the candidate tells you how much learning took place from these experiences, take it one step further to see if the candidate really did learn.
- "How did you *apply* that knowledge (or skill, or information, or insight)?"

The Most Powerful Question

Everyone seems to have his or her favorite, knock-'em-out, separate-the-wheat-from-the-chaff zinger question. But the most powerful and instructive question in the employment interview—whether for technical knowledge or the personal qualities components—is simply this: Why?

When you ask, "Why?" (or its equivalents, "For what reason?", "What was the basis for that?", and so on), you probe way beyond the superficial recall of robot-like action. You get at the candidate's judgment, understanding, decision-making process, values, biases, and so on. This one-word question will reveal more to you than all the zingers you can throw at an applicant.

Fair and Legal

Certainly you want to be fair to your applicants, treating all with respect and an equivalent approach in consideration and assessment. That said, the interview process in particular can be a legal mine field. Please see the next chapter for some important words about employment practices and the law.

GETTING TO THE TARNISH BENEATH THAT SHINE

Do some candidates seem just too good to be true? Do they have all the answers you could only dream of hearing? Probe those ideal responses and pounce on any self-serving assertions such as these:

- "I want to be challenged." ("What exactly do you mean *challenged*? What would be too much challenge? When have you had to handle too much challenge? What did you learn from that? So what, if anything, do you do differently now? How do you know where your limits are? What are the danger signs when you're exceeding the limit?")
- "I'm creative." ("How do you know? Don't you find that can be a liability in executing a defined process? How do you express your creativity? When has your creativity gotten you in trouble? How do you flex your creative muscles when the job doesn't afford you much opportunity for that sort of thing? Can't the creative urge be a distraction and detract from what needs to get done now?")
- "I'm a people person." ("Great! I've always wanted to know what that means. What does it mean to you? When did you discover you were a people person? Have you worked in the past where your people needs weren't met? How much of a people person are you? What was the most intense people experience you've had in the workplace (or a volunteer situation, or school)? When have you had your fill of people? In an average day, how much people contact—in terms of minutes or hours—did you have?")
- "I'm totally driven by this kind of work." ("Really? What do you mean by that? Does that mean I should expect you to

always be available for meeting the insane deadlines requiring nights and weekends? How long could you keep that up and maintain the quality we demand? Can you imagine an entire career like that? Isn't that a little one-dimensional? Where is the burnout point for you? What are you doing about maintaining a balanced perspective? We get a little concerned about people who burn out prematurely; how do you know that won't happen to you?")

- "I'm customer-focused." ("How focused? How do you know? What was the last customer complaint you handled? What do you do when you disappoint a customer? Why would you disappoint a customer, and how does that happen? How many times has that happened? How do you stay in tune with customer preferences? How do you know when they're changing? How do you gauge customer satisfaction? What's an acceptable failure rate? Do you deliver perfection? How do you know if your customer focus is good enough? When was the last time you changed a process in response to customer feedback?")
- "I always deliver." ("Wow! Always? Why do you think that is? Who could I speak to who could verify such an extraordinary record of accomplishment? Haven't you had a few missteps along the way? Tell me about a few of them.")

Every "strength" has its dark side. Probe the candidate's claims to find out if he knows this and has wrestled with it. If he hasn't, he may not have the quality he thinks he does, or it has not matured to be the asset he would like to present it as. If you get stuck for a way to turn the assertion back at the candidate, gently ask this question: "If you had to prove that claim, what real evidence could you offer?"

On the flip side, take with the proverbial grain of salt the oft-repeated hiring advice to be wary of any candidate who says anything negative about a former boss or employer. Hold on! If they were so perfectly happy there, what are they doing here interviewing for a job? Don't automatically discredit "negative" comments. Explore them. Negative emotions tend to run deeper and fiercer than positive ones. What upset a candidate about there is going to hold true here. When you hit that nerve, you open a direct path to the applicant's value system.

Bear down, drill in, and tap that wellspring of insight. The candidate may well be representing the shortcomings of his or her former employer. There surely is no shortage of knuckleheads supervising others and making frustrating, keeping-someone-from-doing-their-best-work policies. The more you explore the frustrations, the more you'll know about what makes that applicant tick and what drives him or her to get up and go or to call in sick.

That said, *do* reject *blamers*. If you hear a pattern of whining or bitter complaints about how *"they* wouldn't do this," and "they kept me from doing that," and "I *would* have if *they* had let me," and other defensive, "yeah, but" excuses, cut the interview. People carrying debilitating chips on their shoulders or knives in their hearts and psyches won't miraculously lose them when they join your payroll. Once a blamer, always a blamer. You've been warned.

Grounding Candidates with "Levelers"

An enthusiastic or confident or apparently superbly competent candidate is showing very solidly. You sense nothing but sincerity. Still, you want to, *need* to, explore his or her limitations and inevitable human failings in a way that is respectful and not off-putting. Enter the "leveler" question. This straightforward approach helps you to balance the scales by simply asking for examples of less-than-perfect performance. Such questions give you an idea of how the candidate copes with and learns from less-than-stellar performance.

"You are clearly an accomplished person. Share with me, if you would, a time when you really screwed up." Or, "Recount a time when you tried but could not

- meet a goal,
- finish an assignment or project,

- please a customer,
- get along with a colleague or coworker,
- achieve a quality standard,
- beat a deadline, or
- perform to expectation."

Follow up with four questions:

- "Why did that happen?"
- "Could you have prevented it?"
- "What did you learn?"
- "Have you had a similar experience since then?"

INTERVIEWS: VALID AND RELIABLE?

There's something of a terribly strange paradox in the everyday practice of employment law. Makers of employment tests must be prepared to prove to a court of law the reliability and non-discriminatory nature—in terms of impact on the scores of various protected classes—of the instruments they produce (see previous chapter). But it seems interviewers can ask all kinds of questions and draw any number of bizarre, ill-founded, or even irrational conclusions about a candidate with apparent impunity. That is, as long as they don't commit the cardinal sin of asking about age, race, national origin, religious beliefs, marital status, sexual preference, or whatever else the government feels can unfairly single out for potential victimization someone who's selling his or her skills on the open market. Doesn't that seem strange?

> *A question not asked is a door not opened.*
> —Marilee C. Goldberg
> Counselor and Author

Most employment interviews, studies show, have a low predictive validity factor. In other words, every time you interview someone whom you hire but who then leaves in a short period of time (say within a year) for a reason other than death, retirement, or family relocation, it is arguably evidence of the interview's

Interviewing: "So, Tell Me About Myself" 175

failure to accurately predict success in the job. After all, if the match were so good, why would the "qualified" candidate-turned-employee not be there a mere year later?

Despite the provable failure of job interviews to validly and reliably predict future performance, they are a rite of passage to the payroll that few managers could imagine giving up, and many would fight to keep them despite the associated hassles. Never mind that they don't know how to do it, verifiably don't do it well, and do it with results few would brag about. They *know* they can read an applicant—and better than any psychobabble test can, they'll have you know!

So why isn't there the scrutiny of the employment interview that there is of the employment test? It is perplexing. Think of how odd a proposition it is to claim that a test discriminates, that it has an unfair *adverse impact* on members of a particular group. Could a paper-and-pencil test possibly know the skin color, accent, faith, or lifestyle of the person completing it? Could it care?

Isn't there a far greater likelihood that unfair adverse impact would occur in an employment interview? Take the case of a hiring manager who loves a candidate's résumé, test scores, and reference reports until he lays eyes on the person. He sees that Terry is a *she*, and she's... *not* white! Amazingly, the otherwise highly qualified Terry "blows" the interview. Seems she just didn't "come across with the necessary confidence and communication skills we were looking for."

When called to the witness stand to defend that judgment, what would that manager's criteria for such a determination look like?

Expect more legal activity surrounding the validity and reliability of what is arguably (and probably provably) the weakest link in the assessment chain. Lawsuits in which test validity is called into question are, ironically, easier to win *because* there is science behind many of the tests. You can't prove a negative and you can't indict and convict what you can't point to. Try to prove someone was not fair and did not want to help his employer—and his own career—by hiring a truly qualified person because the invisible, immeasurable qualities of prejudice, bias, and bigotry prevented him from making the self-interested business judgment he is paid to make. Proving that such a twisted logic prevails in the deep recesses of an employment interviewer's head is a lot tougher than, say, citing reams of meta-analyses to prove—or calling only-too-eager expert witnesses to testify—that any given employment test is imperfect.

But never underestimate the creativity or will or chutzpah of plaintiff's lawyers seeking to right the world's wrongs. Protect yourself, and the integrity of your interviewing process, by having the following:

1. A clear, defensible, "business purpose" basis for the nontechnical, personal attributes that you probed for and decided were necessary in a candidate (use the Job Profile Matrix and the process that underlies it to determine and justify such essential capacities);
2. specific criteria for describing what was minimally acceptable in demonstrating the presence of the personal qualities you needed in the person filling the job (use the Key Qualifications Profile with clear, definitive evidentiary descriptions under "Demonstrated by...");
3. evidence that those qualities were fairly assessed, such as a completed Candidate Assessment Grid with the necessary documentation to support it or a structured interview that asks the same core, competence-related questions of all candidates, with notes from each interview—completed during and *immediately* following the interview—and indications of how you reached your conclusions about whether there was a match between the candidate's responses and the requisite competency standards; and
4. data you've gathered since implementing your hiring system that provide evidence about how the people hired under it have improved the company's results in terms of a job's higher productivity levels with a new hire; the lower initial turnover of new hires; the longer-term tenure; and

the better sales, customer satisfaction, quality, and other measures attributable to the work done by hires of higher quality.

Finally, recognize that the Terrys of the world can actually blow their interviews. This may happen to the great disappointment of managers who are committed to diversifying their companies' employee bases. Such managers may genuinely and eagerly welcome qualified candidates in Terry's demographic group, but not at the expense of these individuals not being able to perform at acceptable levels. Hiring a insufficiently-capable person in a protected class out of fear of reprisal, or because of social pressure, or misguided altruism (do you do anyone a favor by setting them up to fail?) carries a greater risk of far worse consequences for the organization and applicant than justifiably rejecting an applicant on sound principle.

Hire people truly suited to doing carefully defined jobs. Follow a good process. Make sound judgments. Sleep well at night.

Bias and Prejudice Behind the Interviewer's Desk

Face-to-face interviewing brings us straight into the face of our own shortcomings. We are all captives of our personal prisons of biases. We make premature and often unfounded judgments about people because of how they appear to us. He really needs to get his dental work done. She's wearing too much (or not enough) makeup. That sari or that yarmulke or those cornrows really aren't proper workplace attire. That jewelry is too flashy. I can't trust someone who doesn't look you straight in the eye. He said, 'his companion'; he's probably some kind of weirdo. That posture surely reflects low self-esteem. That name is too cumbersome for a sales rep to use while calling on customers. Anyone whose accent sounds like that surely can't be too bright. And on it goes.

For most of us, the most common and most seemingly benign of our prejudices is that we tend to ascribe higher value to people who seem much like ourselves, and lower value to those who don't. Some of those similarities and differences are subtle: pace of movement, voice inflection, shared geographic origins, similar taste in books or music or movies, common alma mater, and so on. Others are more blatant: age, accent, skin color, and outward signs of religious faith. It is a trap and a fallacy to define competence or qualification by "looking in the mirror."

The challenge is to recognize one's biases. At the core of our biases is an assumption: People like me are probably good; people who aren't...well, who knows? Such an assumption sounds harsh and unfair. That's the funny thing about assumptions—they're almost always silent and invisible, like carbon monoxide gas. And they can be just as deadly. Even "positive" prejudices can be bad. That minority group is smarter than most. This one makes for better police officers, bridge workers, lawyers… Those "not negative" statements may not seem harmful, but they are as unfair to those included by their bias as they are to those excluded by it.

It is said that what we don't know can kill us. Just as assuredly, what we don't admit to ourselves can poison our actions.

Consider this personal case in point, the principle of which applies to any of those prejudices mentioned above (and many others too numerous to list). I grew up in a multi-ethnic inner-city neighborhood during the racial strife of the mid-1960s. There were multiple ethnic populations living next door to each other. While many black children lived on my block, none went to the parochial school I attended. I saw these children, and occasionally experienced an unpleasant "encounter" with one or two of them, like I did with all kinds of other kids, but never knew any of them.

Growing up in that turbulent, divisive period of racial tension, I was aware of differences, oblivious to similarities, and absolutely sure I was not a biased, racist bigot. After all, I regularly, joyfully, and admiringly listened to the "soul" station on the radio. I was in awe of and filled with deep admiration for the Rev. Dr. Martin Luther King, Jr. (one of the very few people, contemporary or otherwise, whom I consider a personal hero). Still, unknown to me for even decades later, I was, despite my certainty of harboring no bias, prejudicial in that I had formed assumptions about a group of "others" I had been near but did not personally know.

My assumptions and their offspring, prejudices, became apparent to me only many years later. That's when I realized that the black people I had come to know and respect and care for were not like the images—formed by prejudices—I had silently held in my mind's eye for so many years. Only after too long a time did I feel the nagging tug of the slowly emerging and uncomfortable dissonance between my experience and the prejudices that I didn't realize I had (and would have died denying). Eventually, I recognized and admitted that I had made a faulty assumption, however seemingly benign, that had lain silent.

It was easy to overlook. I did nothing "prejudicial." I didn't discriminate against any black person, having both hired and promoted colleagues of color. But my bias found voice whenever I would describe to a friend or family member some mundane story of the day. I wouldn't say, "One of the people said…" but rather, "A black man who was there said…" I defined people by their visible but irrelevant difference. On its face, that's not a terrible offense—and that's the problem. Such a seemingly innocuous thing can be quietly limiting without drawing any attention to itself.

Seeing past apparent differences to peer into the less visible or even invisible attributes of another first requires us to tear down the impenetrable albeit invisible screen of our own prejudices, biases, and wickedly tacit assumptions. The first step in this personal rehabilitation is to spend some quiet and frightening moments penetrating the protective vault around our deepest, most intimate secrets, those that we keep hidden even from ourselves. Only after looking in the mirror and knowing that you see a biased person there can you move past the prejudice to see another person for who they really are.

The Interview Process

Candidates should be evaluated in multiple interviews by multiple interviewers, all of whom are aware of and are provided information regarding the required capacities and competence indicators. Notes made during the interviews should be evaluated for evidence of the required and desired competence and values, and assessments for each candidate should be entered onto the Candidate Assessment Grid.

Interviews should sound more like a conversation than an interrogation, but they are more than a friendly exchange of information. The Natural Selection Hiring Method counts interviewing as an essential information-gathering tool when it is conducted as a sequence of planned, structured, consistent, and fair probes into representations made by a candidate, as shown on Figure 8-1 (page 181).

Great Beginnings and Endings

Begin the interview by advising the candidate of the unusual interview ahead. Urge him or her not to tell you what he or she thinks you want to hear.

> "We're delighted that you're interested in working here. We really need to know who each other really is to get a sense of the potential fit between you, this particular job, and this company. You'll spend more waking hours working here than

Interviewing: "So, Tell Me About Myself" 181

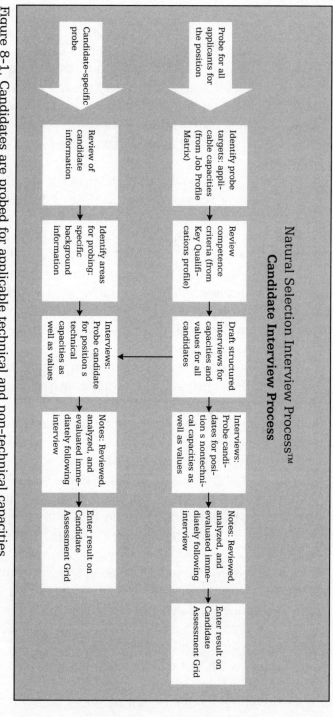

Figure 8-1. Candidates are probed for applicable technical and non-technical capacities as well as values in multiple interviews.

doing anything else in your life. We both owe it to you to see if this is a good fit—to keep your stress level lower and your career prospects higher. Does that make sense to you?

"I'm going to ask you many questions today. There are no 'right' answers and no 'wrong' answers to my questions. I promise that I am not going to give you any 'trick' questions or do anything to intentionally raise your stress level. I want you to relax and have a good experience here today. Are you relaxed?

"I want you to know that some of the questions I'll ask you today may seem a bit unusual just because they're not the standard, 'tell me about yourself' interview questions. Understand that I won't ask you anything that's not truly important to your performance on this job. I absolutely will not ask you anything that is inappropriate or an invasion of your privacy. I simply want to get to know the real you. I will also be copletely candid with you about what the job, the company, and your prospective boss are all really like—warts and all. Does that sound fair?

"So you'll 'give it to me straight' and not try to 'psych out' any questions by trying to tell me what you think I want to hear? Great, because if you take this job, it's the real you who's going to come here every day. And it's the real you who we're going to keep or fire for non-performance. I don't want to hire someone only to turn around and fire him because he's not the person he represented himself to be in the hiring process. I want to find a great fit so that the person who takes this job is well suited to it, jumps right in, has a ball doing it, and produces great work. Does that make sense?

"A suggestion I'd make to you is to answer my questions with the same candor that I'd expect to hear if I were to call your references and ask them the same questions about you. By the way, you are aware that we do an extensive reference and background check, right?

"Great. Ready to begin? OK. First, do you have any questions that you want to ask me before I start asking you questions? Well then, tell me about yourself..."

Of course, some written version of this (perhaps even to be signed by the prospective employee) could be made part of the application process and then briefly referenced before the actual interview took place.

Multiple Inquisitions

A thorough review of a candidate means several interviews, conducted by you and others. Never push for ninety minutes or more. You might want to "wear down" the applicant, but you'll be worn down, too. Plan no fewer than three interviews: a technical or work history review, a reveal-the-person interview, and interviews by others. Remember that many executives swear that peer interviews are more revealing and have higher predictive validity than other types. "They're tougher on the candidate and can smell a phony faster," as one senior human resource executive put it.

Another effective technique is to have the candidate interview with people at multiple organizational levels. Some people "defer up" quite convincingly, and are total jerks to people they perceive as being of lower status. Many classic stories circulate in employment circles about the executive or pilot or doctor who played well to senior management and peers but was dismissive or disrespectful to a receptionist—or an executive posing as one. Such behavior reveals the true self and is absolutely just cause for pulling the plug on an otherwise "qualified" candidate.

Interviews both take time and need to move fast. In a tight labor market, good candidates are sometimes snatched up in days. That's all the more reason to adhere to a defined process such as the Natural Selection Hiring Method to standardize the procedure and speed decision-making.

Is the investment of time worthwhile? Well, would you get married after one date? You'll likely see as much or more of your new hire than you do of your spouse. Don't you want more than the most superficial impression of who they really are? Is your partner the same person he or she appeared to be on your first date?

At the conclusion of the interview, always ask the candidate, "Was there anything I didn't ask you about that you would like me to know?" and, "What questions do you have of me?" Thank the candidate for his or her time and candor. Then explain the next step in the process and the time interval between now and then.

Getting Expert Help

There's no more important work or better use of your time than investing in getting the right people on board to fulfill your organization's mission. That said, it is also fair and accurate to say that completing a job profile, planning an appropriate assessment scheme, structuring an effective job interview, preparing interview questions that draw from an applicant the information you really feel you need to make a good hiring decision, and otherwise executing the Natural Selection Hiring Method take a chunk of time.

Here are three thoughts on that:

1. This is what it takes to really zero in on people who are best suited to successfully executing the work and fulfilling the mission of your organization.
2. Because it's a big job, many of your competitors may also resist doing it. Therein lies your opportunity for competitive advantage. If you ever said, "Our people make the difference," here's the opportunity to make that statement a reality.
3. You need not go it alone. There are resources that can help you. Right within your own company you may have some underutilized employment experts. In addition, there are many consultants and freelancers who can help you administer a better-structured, more effective employment process. You can rent people to de-

vise questions and structure interviews; tailor competency descriptions and assessment measures; do some interviewing of candidates; observe, track, and report on simulation performance; and help with all the aspects we've discussed to this point.

Get the assistance you need so that you really do execute according to plan.

Shrink Squeeze

If you want to design and validate your own assessment processes or create instruments for use in your company or beyond, there are independent, consulting industrial/organizational (I/O) psychologists who can assist you (although, interestingly, there are not very many in proportion to the number of industries and organizations in the U.S.). The Society of Industrial and Organizational Psychology, or SIOP, a division of the American Psychological Association based in Washington, DC, has a membership of only 2,500. That includes those who make their living in academia and at major corporations such as AT&T. SIOP estimates the number of psychologists who are not among their members but are doing organizational consulting at only another 2,500. That adds up to a total of 5,000 across the entire U.S. That's a pretty rare breed, with thin coverage for even just tending to the Fortune 500.

Part Three
Other Important Information for Employment Deployment

Chapter Nine
Staying Out of Hiring
Manager's Prison: Legalities

Chapter Ten
Long-Term Relationships:
Recruiting and Retention

Chapter Nine

Staying Out of Hiring Manager's Prison: Legalities

> From a legal perspective, it is harder to discharge employees than to select them.
> —Personnel Systems & Technologies Corp. Web site

Hiring is not exactly a private matter. There are laws governing what you can and can't do. These laws were passed to protect individuals from discrimination and to imbue the process with some sense of fairness. Briefly, here's what you've got to know about the legal issues in hiring:

1. Do not do *anything* that results in discrimination against individuals on the basis of race, color, sex, age, religion, national origin or citizenship (unless the candidate is an illegal alien), veteran's status, pregnancy, marital status, sexual preference, arrests without conviction, medical conditions not related to job performance, performance on tests not related to job performance, educational creden-

tials not necessary for job performance, or imperfections for which reasonable accommodation would enable one to perform the job.
2. Staying legal in your employment practices requires vigilance, patience, and a tolerance for ambiguity.

You need vigilance because the applicable employment case law can evolve on a moment's notice. You need patience and tolerance because staying in compliance for even the most conscientious, upright corporate citizen can be thwarted by contradictory policies between various federal agencies, vague statutory language in well-meaning but somewhat confused laws, and case law that varies by jurisdiction and, seemingly, time of day. In that environment, you need to rely not on this or any other book but on an employment lawyer who can counsel based on current conditions.

Before I launch into a litany of *don't do this* and *don't do that*, here's a little perspective. While everyone rightfully pays attention to the occasionally mind-numbingly confusing and conflicting employment policies dictated by law, it is worth noting that the federal employment police are unlikely to either kick in or padlock your company doors because someone thought you looked cross-eyed at them in a job interview. In early 1998 the EEOC had a 65,000-case backlog, even though it receives fewer than six claims per 10,000 workers annually (while employment in the U.S. is at full tilt, the number of claims filed is *decreasing*).

In the fall of 1997, *U.S. News & World Report* noted that in 1996 alone, more than 23,000 suits alleging race, sex, disability, or age discrimination were filed in federal courts, more than double the 1992 total of 10,771. But, the magazine reported, "given the number of employed Americans, currently at a record 129.7 million (eleven million more than in 1992), the number of people who actually take legal action is minuscule."

Am I suggesting you flout the law because both the risk and the enforcement are a little thin? No. I am suggesting that you put employment law concerns in proper perspective.

In addition to the case load backlog at EEOC, it is interesting to note that, despite the occasional headline-grabbing case about a discriminatory practice at a corporate behemoth, most of the cases turn out to be frivolous complaints. This is borne out statistically and by the EEOC's own admission that it doesn't do a good job on the intake end of the process, accepting almost every case where someone charges, "I've been wronged, I've been wronged!" On the statistical side of the scorecard, a mere 4 to 5% of all EEOC cases actually find "cause" against the employer. Fifteen to 20% of cases are settled, and 70 to 80% get dropped, according to Mary-Jane Sinclair, managing partner of a New Jersey-based human resources consulting firm.

Furthermore, a mid-1997 study commissioned by the Society for Human Resource Management (SHRM) found that of all employment-related lawsuits, a very small percentage actually involved *hiring*. It wasn't employment applicants but *former employees* who filed the vast majority—80%—of employment-related lawsuits; 14% were filed by a company's current employees, while a meager 3% were brought by unsuccessful candidates for employment.

You don't want to be negligent or careless in your hiring practices, but you should remain shy of complete paranoia in your level of vigilance. Again, when in doubt, talk to an attorney who specializes in employment law.

"I Wouldn't Do That"

When in doubt, consult your attorney—wise words to be sure. But they beg for a little additional perspective. Ever ask your lawyer, "Is it OK for us to do such-and-such?" What did the lawyer reply? Did she say, "Sure, absolutely, no problem, go right ahead"?

A lawyer's job is to reduce risk, both for her client, and—you need to know—for her law firm. When you ask, "Can we do this?" the following little question pops into your attorney's mind: "What could happen to me if I said 'yes'?" You see, lawyers don't want to give you permission to do anything with even the remotest chance of negative repercussions. Your company could be sued, and if it is sued after you acted on the advice of counsel, you might just turn the tables and launch a malpractice action of your own against your trusted legal advisor. So there's plenty of reason for your lawyer to "just say no."

Without question, it is prudent business practice to make sure that your procedures and practices are legally sound. If you ask your lawyer whether it is legally acceptable to do such-and-such and your lawyer says no, ask why. Ask him or her to cite the appropriate statute or case law. If your lawyer can't produce evidence of any prohibitive legal precedent, ask him or her to provide a risk analysis. You already know that nothing in life that is worth doing is risk-free. Is your lawyer advising you not to do something because you're facing a half-percent risk or a 97 percent risk? What is the basis for the assessment?

There's a difference between avoiding a known risk and simply doing nothing at all. No progress ever came from simply doing nothing at all—and often there is a great risk to that, too.

Key Do's and Don'ts

Do
- Treat all candidates with respect and fairness.
- Process and assess candidates in an equal and consistent manner.
- Give every candidate every opportunity to succeed in the process.
- Keep records and notes related to your assessments.
- Use methods that are strictly related to predicting performance success on the job.

Staying Out of Hiring Manager's Prison: Legalities

Don't
- Do not ask in writing (for example, on an employment application) or verbally for information that would reveal an applicant's
  - race,
  - color,
  - sex (unless it's a bona fide occupational requirement),
  - age,
  - religion,
  - national origin,
  - pregnancy status,
  - marital/family status,
  - sexual preference,
  - arrest record without conviction,
  - discharge status from armed services (it is OK to ask if the candidate received a dishonorable discharge),
  - medical conditions not related to job performance,
  - performance on tests not related to job performance,
  - educational credentials not necessary for job performance,
  - physical or mental imperfections that are not related to the job (see below),
  - financial situation or history (unless a bond is required),
  - native language,
  - use of birth control or family planning,
  - membership in a labor organization, or
  - memberships in social clubs or organizations that are not job-related.

ABOUT DISABILITIES

The ADA prohibits discrimination against people with a disability that, with "reasonable accommodation," would not render one incapable of performing the job duties. In other words, if a little effort on your part would allow an otherwise fit-for-the-job disabled person to do the work, you can't deny him an employment opportunity. Here's an example: An applicant for a telemarketing job is a superb candidate, but his wheelchair doesn't fit in the standard cubicle configuration assigned to telemarketers. Not hiring your otherwise-qualified candidate for that minor reason could be unfair discrimination because with a reasonable accommodation (maybe a couple hundred dollars in modifications to the workstation) you could hire the candidate and enable him to perform the job. The ADA requires that an employer provide a reasonable accommodation as long as it does not cause an undue hardship to the firm. (What is *reasonable*? What is *undue hardship*? What do you think we have courts for?)

How do you ask a candidate about potentially disqualifying disabilities—those that would prohibit effective execution of the job's responsibilities—without running afoul of the law? Ask him or her, "This job involves performing the following tasks... If you were hired to do this job, could you perform those tasks with or without reasonable accommodation?"

Here are two closing thoughts. First, remember this: When in doubt, consult a qualified legal advisor. Second, as *U.S. News & World Report's* Amy Saltzman so perfectly puts it, "The best way to avoid legal trouble is to run a fair-minded, well-managed business that doesn't waste too much energy worrying about getting sued."

Chapter Ten

Long-Term Relationships: Recruiting and Retention

> Here lies a man who attracted better people into his service than he was himself.
> —Inscription that industrialist
> Andrew Carnegie wanted on his tombstone

American Airlines hired some 1,500 welfare recipients, and, in the process, reduced its company-wide recruitment costs by twenty percent. Marriott, UPS, Blockbuster Video, and other major companies also have started to fill open positions with unemployed people who are swapping their welfare checks for paychecks.

There's a labor shortage. The baby bust, coupled with a boom economy, has companies scrambling for hired help. Many are turning to unusual sources and tactics to fill job openings.

IBM, in search of new employees, trolled for talent on a Florida beach during spring break. Recruiters hoped to turn college students' attention from playing in the ocean blue going to work for Big Blue. Up the coast in New York, an ad agency is paying a bounty of $1,000 a head to employees who bring in new blood. Texas Instruments pays $1,500 for referring a new engineering employee. Other high-tech firms are knocking heads not in the open market but in dark, windowless hotel ballrooms; they're staffing at "job fairs." Speaking of hotels, at the Hyatt in Orlando, Florida, where the unemployment rate hovers at about three percent, the "back of the house" work is getting done by 100 new employees recently imported from Lithuania, the Czech Republic, and Russia. They're coming to America to do laundry, make beds, polish brass, and peel potatoes. Also in Florida, Disney is shipping in recruits from Puerto Rico for help in its Florida parks.

As high-tech and service companies were scrambling to find workers at both ends of the skills scale, Andersen Consulting ran a full-page ad in the Sunday *New York Times*, three quarters of which was a picture of a boy, dressed up as a caped crusader, standing next to his dog. The headline beneath the photo read, "You wanted to save the world. Would you settle for helping a few global companies?" "Bring your life experiences to us," coos the ad in its plea to attract people who want to change the world by becoming consultants.

A 1997 survey of human resource executives by the Society for Human Resource Management identified the average HR manager's top employment challenge as finding candidates (followed by retaining those hired and selecting those best qualified). Every company in America, it seems, is desperately seeking somebody to take its money. Well, not quite. Southwest Airlines, an uncommonly successful regional air carrier, gets 150,000 résumés a year but hires a mere 5,000, "an admissions policy that's Ivy League stingy," sniffs *Fortune* magazine.

Southwest has a secret weapon in the war for talent: Its employees. They love the joint. Meet one off the job and listen to him gush about the exciting environment. The energy. The fun. The *fun*? Oh, yes, the fun. You simply *cannot* get Southwest to hire you unless you're fun. They absolutely screen for it and celebrate "fun" as a core corporate value. All those happy, fun-loving people enjoy working together, and their customers sense it and keep coming back because of it. Southwest customers tell other people about that swinging airline that won't give you a bag of peanuts to save your life, but what a *great bunch of people*! The word spreads. People who aren't having a swinging good time at work (perhaps because they're chasing recruits in dark hotel ballrooms) catch wind of this "Southwest thing." They want in, too. Somehow, without dropping big bucks on full-page ads or combing beaches, Southwest is drawing talent—and it's the only major U.S. air carrier that has been profitable every year for more than two decades.

MAGNET RECRUITING

The best recruiting campaign is an ongoing one. It is staffed by everyone on the payroll. It relies on the magnet pull of a great— not *OK*, but *great*—place to work. Nothing attracts good people like a satisfied, motivated workforce.

At a dinner meeting I attended with some people from a client company that has a great reputation among its employees, one new employee relayed a recent conversation she had with a friend. Her friend, upon learning that the new employee had just joined this company, exclaimed, "What happened—did somebody die and create an opening?" Companies that really do treat employees as valued *human assets*—by appealing to their human interests as well as financial needs—tend to spend less time worrying about attracting more humans to the payroll, even when they're expanding. (They don't need to fret about retention, either.)

Magnet recruiting is powered by reputation, which is fueled by word of mouth. That kind of advertising costs nothing, works constantly, and is the most credible of all. A strong reputation as a great place to work expands the number of people who would even think about your company as a potential employer. That expands your available labor pool, which in turn increases your chances for finding top talent.

Ongoing magnet recruiting is critical for two reasons: First, open positions cost a company productivity, profits, and opportunities (sometimes to the point where the company must turn away business because it simply doesn't have the people it needs to support it); and second, position recruiting costs significant money. (The Employment Management Association has been tracking cost per hire for better than a dozen years. It estimates overall cost per hire at well over $3,000, while the cost per hire for professional and managerial personnel is more than $6,000 a head.)

Recruiting the old-fashioned way, going out for people instead of having them come to you, costs money. But ironically, those expenses are often incurred to fill openings created by people who left the organization for reasons other than money. A late 1997 survey released by Coopers & Lybrand, the professional services firm, reveals that nearly forty percent of employee turnover is for reasons other than money.

Psychic paychecks count considerably in creating an environment where people want to stay, and where they happily do their best work. Interestingly, the Coopers & Lybrand analyst who reviewed the survey's results, partner Carl Weinberg, weighed in with this apropos conclusion: "In our experience, there is usually a significant gap between the expectations of the employment deal that the employer created and the reality of the job. This gap weakens commitment and pushes good people out the door." In other words, people mismatched to their jobs would rather quit than retrofit (see Chapter 1).

LURING THE FISH FROM THE SEA

If you must troll for talent until the good word spreads far and fast enough, here are some techniques you might find helpful.

Pay your employees as recruiters. If they're not selling your shop on sheer enthusiasm, add some cash to the mix. Increasingly, companies are offering stipends for referring potential employees. Many companies stagger the bounty: They pay about a third when the applicant clears the first interview, another payment when the candidate becomes an employee, and the balance when the new employee completes his or her first six months or year on the payroll. Employees who refer others and have a stake in the future success of their referrals tend to send good people to the personnel office. To get employees interested in recruiting, publicize your bounty. *Often.* People forget, so keep the recruiting campaign at the top of their minds.

Provide employees with recruiting business cards. ("Good opportunities for good people." List the recruiting line telephone number on the front of the card and the benefits on the back.) And don't forget to encourage nepotism. Extended family members often work well together in team environments; their unvarnished candor can bring peer pressure to bear in a most productive way.

Go where the new recruits are (even if you've never been there before). Some state employment or welfare agencies have employment coordinators, facilities, and budgets for training; some can provide tax rebates for companies that help people move from welfare rolls to payrolls (or help the disabled move into productive livelihoods). Call some agencies. Start working the bureaucracy to open a new pipeline of talent. Some companies also have had success working with community groups that sponsor job fairs and insert recruiting fliers into welfare check envelopes. You might be pleasantly surprised to learn that many people on welfare have had good prior working experience until fate threw them a curve (see a brief discussion of bias in Chapter 8). Poverty is neither terminal nor contagious, so don't overlook this potential source of help.

Go where the "less-new" recruits are. Many older workers might be coaxed back for part-time work if someone would just ask. Don't expect them to respond to your fliers or bulletin board postings. They don't *need* the work, and might feel guilty about displacing a young worker—until you assure them they shouldn't. Go to the senior center. Explain their opportunities and your needs. *Display* your enthusiasm, and you might just catch a recruit or two or ten. Also, contact your state or regional office of the American Association of Retired Persons (AARP). The national organization doesn't involve itself with placing older workers, but some of the local affiliates do.

Hire part of a company. For some professional posts in accounting, advertising, secretarial services, software development, and even HR, consider an arrangement with a local consultant, freelancer, or business owner. Buy a few days a week or month. You may get higher-level, more productive talent for the same or less money than a regular full-time employee would cost, all with no benefit expenses.

Catch 'em on the rebound. Watch the business section for announcements of businesses large and small that are consolidating, moving, or closing. Some good people will be displaced. Get to them first and talk to them about opportunities with your company. Establish a relationship with local or regional military operations. People leaving military service are disciplined, trained, used to hard work, and ready for the next chapter in their career (not to mention the fact that they are already accustomed to bad coffee and doing a lot to earn their pay).

Open your doors. Have an open house. Give tours. Give away goodies. Have a picnic, ice cream party, or community art contest. Get more people to know who you are. Offer a "fast start" bonus to the first X number of people hired. Invite the media. Even if none of the people who attend your event sign up to pursue a job, they may know someone who will, or tell someone who will tell someone, and so on. The worst that can happen is that you'll generate a little community goodwill.

Get the word out. Brightly colored fliers, clever billboards, witty public service announcements for the radio—these can all help you stand out and get some response. American Express has even recruited for help with those little ads on the back of supermarket register receipts.

Those radio announcements, by the way, often are *free*. Radio stations often consider them a community service to people who might be looking for work. If you can make the announcement a bit catchy or funny, the radio station may be inclined to use it more frequently. Have your employees enter a "what's good about working at our company" contest, with winners for best slogan and poster design, and all other entrants entered into a drawing for prizes. That boosts morale, gets employees thinking about what's positive at your place, and puts them into a recruiting frame of mind.

Let your customers know you're looking. They already like your company. They may pass the word along to a friend or relative, or may even think about talking to you about employment. Use your regular advertisements to snare new recruits. Down at the bottom, right under your logo, put a message to this effect: *a great company always looking for more great employees*, or *a great place to work, too*, or *growing with great career opportunities*, or *join our winning team and make a difference*, or *be a part of the success story; apply now*, or *great products from great people*, and so on.

Use telephone and computer technology. Set up an automated phone system—the "opportunity hotline"—with details about open posts, benefits, the hiring process, and other appropriate information. Offer more information by fax. Indicate how interested people should contact you. Use the Internet to promote openings. Even if your company doesn't have its own Web site, post job listings on Web services that link technology-savvy hopefuls with potential employers. If you do have a Web site, include a "career opportunities" link and encourage people to e-mail their résumés to you. The Internet extends your reach far beyond your immediate vicinity. It allows people anywhere in the world who are planning to or thinking about or open to the possibility of relocating to your area to learn about your company and its employment opportunities almost effortlessly.

Take raw recruits who earn while they learn. Internships, apprenticeships, and career exploration arrangements with high schools, vocational schools, and community colleges all can offer a supply of self-motivated and interested—though perhaps a little green—potential new employees. Some programs may even help to subsidize wages while you provide on-the-job training. "Growing" your own workers may be a slower ramp up to full productivity, but it can be more productive overall. By developing skills your way from the start, there's less retrofitting. Internship-type programs give you a great opportunity to try-before-you-buy, as recommended in Chapter Six. By developing a close relationship with the guidance and career counselors at the appropriate institutions, you'll have an ex officio (and gratis) recruiting staff that keeps an eye out for talent that's a good fit with your needs (provided they know what your needs are).

Embrace diversity. It snowballs your recruiting. As mentioned above, word of mouth by your employees is a very powerful recruiting mechanism. But it only extends as far as the networks your employees live in. Most communities are collections of fragmented and somewhat insular sub-communities. If you have no employees who live or socialize in the Pakistani, Korean, or Ukrainian communities, you are not wired in to them. They don't know you, and they probably wouldn't think of working for you.

Take a risk with an industry-changer. Capable, competent mid-career managers or professionals sometimes languish after their industry shrinks or their personal dissatisfaction with their profession grows. Most skills for most jobs can be transferred to another industry. Often, however, hiring managers think "industry" before "skills," and this can be a debilitating bias, as damaging to both parties as any other. Unfortunately, this industry bias traps some people in career or industry choices that they made twenty or thirty years ago in their mostly uninformed youth. A 45-year-old person probably decided on—or more likely, stumbled into—his or her profession some 25 years ago. (Perhaps not surprisingly, surveys of mid-career professionals show that many regret their career choices. Many mid-career lawyers, for example, say they would not choose law if they could do it over again.)

Work behaviors from several capacities, such as interpersonal relationships, problem solving, commitment to quality and customer satisfaction, work practices, and so on can be applied just about anywhere. They're transportable to jobs where the individual's interests and commitment line up with the work. "Relevant experience" may be quite irrelevant. Maturity in judgment need not have been developed in the context of the widget industry to be valid; it just needs to be tempered with good information to fuel good decision making.

Very little of the work done in most companies requires a special license reflecting highly specialized knowledge, or a Ph.D. in the industry-specific peculiarities. Most people with sufficient interest, mental ability, and will to learn the fundamentals can close the industry-specific knowledge gap and augment it with their own unique perspective, forged in another arena of endeavor. For example, the "alternate route" for teachers who did not choose education as their college major bears this out. So do numerous examples of people who have managed to successfully make the transition from one industry to another. The irony is that while many mid-level managers are unwilling to hire someone from outside their industry, it's not unusual for them to report to a senior manager who was recruited from outside the firm or industry altogether for the benefit of a fresh perspective! (In fact, in the post-downsizing economy, some 45 percent of job-changing executives and managers are landing jobs in entirely new fields, according to Manchester Partners International.)

Hire a temporary. Sure, it's more expensive on an hourly basis, and there's a premium to pay if you want to make a temporary permanent, but it's fast and flexible. This try-before-you-buy method brings you people who have already been through a screening process and can be "fired" in an instant, guilt-free. Also, it introduces you to talent that you otherwise might not even know existed.

Hire other people's employees. All's fair in love, war, and business. Entice employees from other payrolls to yours. Recruit aggressively. Freely hand out those recruiting business cards. Recruit people away by simply being a better place to come to work.

Remember that a recruiting effort is a marketing campaign. You are selling your company to people you want to attract. Take a few pages from the marketer's playbook. Understand that recruiting cannot be an occasional event. That's like running an ad once and wondering why no one is buying your product. Advertisers talk about *reach* and *frequency*: getting the message to the right people so often and in such compelling ways that it not only registers but prompts *buying behavior*. Staffing one job fair or running a recruitment ad in one newspaper does not constitute a campaign. On a continual basis, communicate the message that your company wants to hire people and offers them a fulfilling opportunity with a good pay and benefits package. Delivering that message occasionally, through one or two communication channels, does not a siren song make. Applicants won't come running and beat the doors down. As important as anything, be in touch with the needs of this target customer group—your potential workforce. Know what they want and expect from an employer in your market. Be aware of the employment offers of your hiring competitors. Offer an attractive package of both fiscal and psychic paychecks to employees—the people, after all, on whom your company must depend for its success.

The Recruiting Paradox

Good recruiting leads to retention, which eliminates the need for recruiting.

Retain for Gain: Keep What You Recruit

Employees who are satisfied stay with their current employer. If turnover is a problem at your firm, something is wrong. Don't stop at symptoms; identify the root cause. Employee defection is the human equivalent of manufacturing's *scrap* and *rework*, and it results in wasted investment and lost productivity. In your exit interviews, press for deeper truths. Deploy employee surveys that get at core business issues rather than just asking, "are you happy?"

To encourage tenure, assure prospective employees that your company is a better place to work. Seriously and honestly evaluate your company's standing on each of the following items in this list of criteria that employees assess when they "hire" an employer:

- *Interesting work.* A job that someone wants to stay in must fit with his or her personal needs, strengths, and values. People in the wrong jobs suffer and then often quit.
- *Clarity of expectations.* When job descriptions are missing, incomplete, or out of date, particularly in terms of the worker's desired outcomes, the employee lacks a sense of purpose. The job has no meaning; the worker is simply doing time. In that case, you've merely rented someone's time, not hired him or her to complete a mission.
- *Performance feedback and sense of accomplishment* in work. Employees want a sense of closure in their work, not just to perform tasks without context. That's what machines and circus seals do (of course, the seals get applause).
- *Sense of contribution or meaning from work.* Anyone on the job is there at the expense of doing anything else. Who wants to mark the erosion of his or her life's limited time by doing nothing of significance? Money is poor compensation for that.
- *Sufficient challenge.* A proper and significant use of one's personal talents, once again, comes down to an appropriate fit with the job.

- *Input into and control over one's work.* Want to boss a machine? Hire one. People all come with brains, and they're just waiting to use them.
- *Feeling fairly treated.* Fairness, equal treatment, and reciprocity count in all work matters. Employees keep score on the quality of work assignments, level of support, day-to-day interactions with colleagues and supervisors, formal evaluations, and pay.
- *Feeling valued,* especially through *discretionary* acts. If your pay and benefits package is the same as everywhere else, you get no points—even if it's good. What matters is what your company does beyond the norm to communicate to employees that they are special and appreciated.
- *Relationship with the boss.* Jerks drive people out the door. Leaders will have people doing most anything, not because they have to but because they want to.
- *Relationships with colleagues in your work society.* Teamwork depends on the relationships between everyone on the team. Shirkers, sourpusses, and users drive their competent colleagues away. Fire bad people to keep good ones.
- *Preferred degree of independence.* Some people thrive in a self-management environment while others simply cannot function without direction. It comes down to fit.
- *Pride in the organization.* People who identify with their employer produce better than those who simply trade their time and work for money. A company that values quality and the satisfaction of its customers has more appeal to good people than one whose practices aren't based on such values. The more people know about the organization, the greater the commitment they are willing to make to it. The less frequent or deep the communication from the company, the easier it is for workers to feel nothing for it—and leave without hesitation. Employment is a *relationship*.
- *Stability of the organization.* Is your company troubled? Lost? Why should people stay?
- *Confidence in the organization's future.* If the financial security of an employee's family depends on that of your com-

pany, expect the employee to closely scrutinize your company's prospects and to act in response to them. Investors sell their stock in a company whose future prospects appear bleak; employees who have no confidence in their company's future divest themselves of it by walking away.
- *Opportunity for growth and development.* The best employees are driven by growth and learning. That's why Chapter 8 insists you test for it. When the learning stops, so does the loyalty.
- *Rewards tied to accomplishments.* Pay must not be arbitrary; it must be related to how much effort one makes or the results one delivers.

There is a demonstrably high correlation between prosperous companies that do not have recruiting problems and the work satisfaction of their employees. This is a happy cycle. It turns out that those happy workers also make their employers more profitable. The Gallup Organization surveyed 55,000 workers to gauge the relationship between company profits and employee attitudes. The study, reported in *Fortune* magazine in January of 1998, found that four attitudes "correlate strongly with higher profits":

1. Workers feel they are given the opportunity to do what they do best every day (better fit, not retrofit);
2. they believe their opinions count;
3. they sense that their fellow workers are committed to quality; and
4. they see a direct connection between their own work and the company's mission.

When people feel that way about their employer, why would they even think of leaving?

Appendix
Attributes of Corporate Culture

In Chapter 3 we reviewed the importance of considering corporate culture in evaluating job candidates. Every organization's culture, its common values, norms, and shared expectations—its way of operating—is a unique combination of many factors. These factors, such as workload, compensation, and predominant management style, tend to exist on a continuum, bounded by extremes.

The diagrams in this appendix show the possible range of cultural conditions in 30 categories. The unique mix of a given organization's specific attributes gives that particular organization its distinctive character. A company's culture may not be uniform in all locations, functional areas, or work units, or at all organizational levels. These cultural norms also may vary over time.

The descriptors presented here are not exhaustive. The intent is to present major distinguishing factors to help you identify the the dominant culture of a given unit or workplace day in and day out.

Appendix: Attributes of Corporate Culture

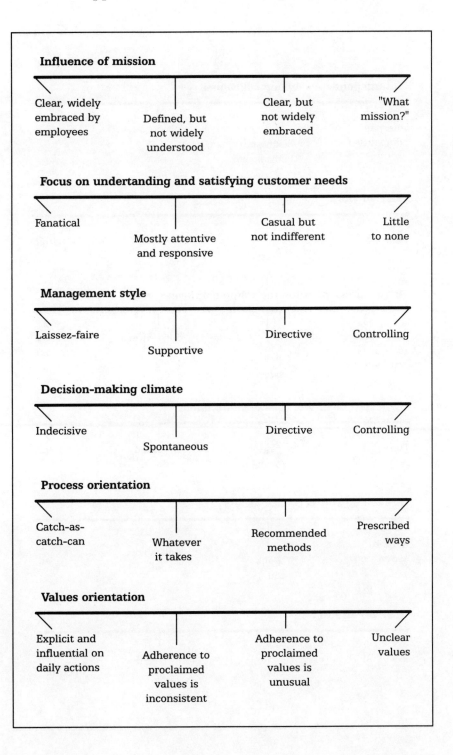

210 Your People *Are* Your Product

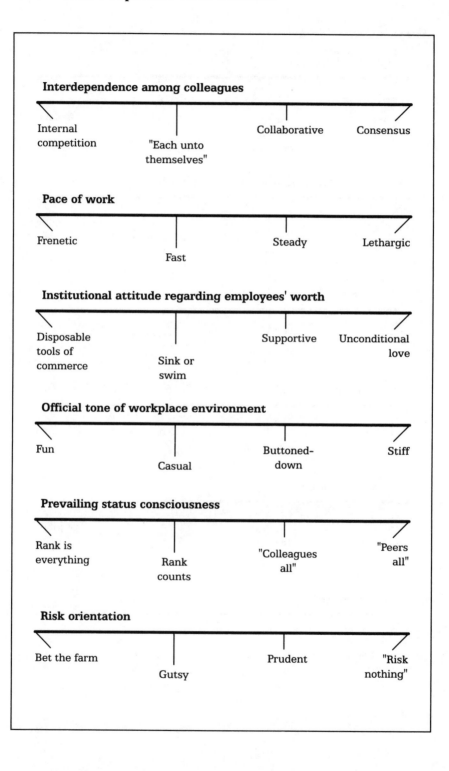

Appendix: Attributes of Corporate Culture

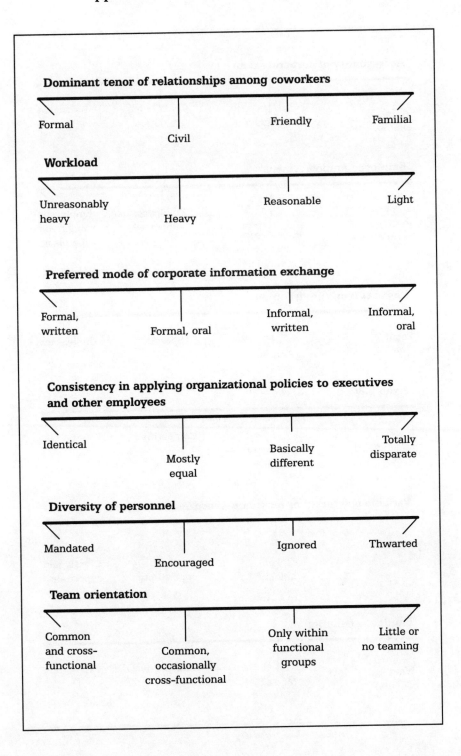

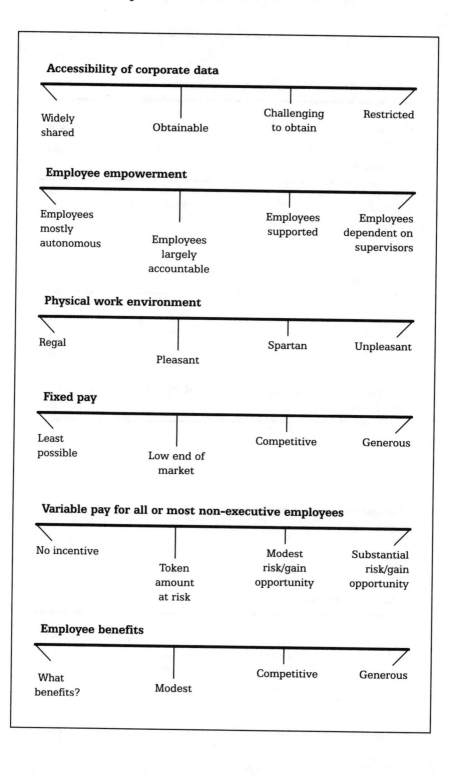

Appendix: Attributes of Corporate Culture

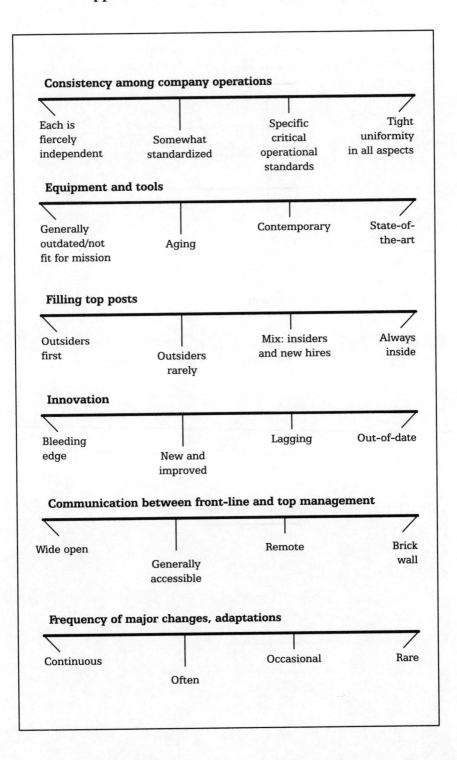

Index

A

Adaptability, 79
Adverse impacts, 175-76
Ambiguity, in assessment, 96-99
American Management Association, 10-11
Americans with Disabilities Act (ADA), 193-97
Analytical capacity, 85
Andersen Consulting, 33-34, 189
Apprenticeships, 194-95
Assessment centers, 108-9
Assessments
    ambiguity in, 96-99
    Candidate Assessment Grid, 122-28
    of candidates' values, 163-71
    flowchart for, 114
    by groups, 127-28, 180
    introduction to, 92-94
    on the job, 102-106
    for key qualifications, 115-22
    labeling in, 926-99
    of references, 111-12, 121-22
    reliability and validity of, 94-96
    simulations, 107-110
    types of, 101
    See also Interviews; Tests
Associated Press, 36
Association of Test Publishers, 132-33
Attitude, and performance, 43-44, 78-79
Attorneys, 195-96
Auditions, 104-106

B

Behavior
    assessing, 97-99, 147-48
    predicting, 95-96, 162-63
    unacceptable, 125, 127, 173, 183-84
    See also Work behaviors
Behavior interviews, 155-63
Behavior-profiling instruments, 97-98. *See also* Personality profiles
Benefits, 212
Bias
    in job interviews, 175-76, 177-80
    in performance reviews, 31-32
Blamers, 173
Bonus qualities, 124-25, 129
Bowes, Lee, 6, 52, 103, 110
Business objectives
    importance to workers, 58, 60
    in organizational culture, 202

C

California Psychological Inventory, 149
Caliper, 148
Candidate assessment. *See* Assessments
Candidate Assessment Grid, 122-28

216   Index

Capability, versus suitability, 48-49
Capacities
  assessing for, 116-22, 122-28
  critical, 126-27, 128-30
  defined, 74-75
  dominant, 47-48
  in Natural Selection Hiring
    Method taxonomy, 74, 78-86
Certified Management
  Consultants, 33
Certified Meeting Professionals, 33
Certified Speaking Professionals,
  33
Change, in organizational culture,
  213
Chemistry, with interviewees, 57-
  58
College degree, as job qualification, 28-32
Communication, in organizational
  culture, 211, 213
Competence
  and credentials, 32-38
  described, 19
  exclusionary rules and, 28-32
  importance of, 24-28, 126-27
  levels of, 70-71, 117-19, 126
  versus qualifications, 20-22
Competitive advantage
  employees as, 3-4
  in interviews, 185
Conceptual capacity, 85
Consultants, prospective
  employees as, 105
Consulting Psychologists Press,
  Inc., 149
Content validity, 137-38. *See also*
  Tests; Validity
Corporate culture.
  attributes of, 208-13
  requirements of, 44, 52-53
Correlation, and test validity, 150-
  51
Credentials
  as job qualification, 32-38, 100
  of testing consultants, 138

Criticality
  in job profiling, 87-89
  of job tasks, 69
  use in candidate assessments,
    124-25
Culture, organizational. *See* Organizational culture
Curiosity, elements of, 79
Customer-focused orientation,
  156, 209
Customer service representatives,
  45-46
Customers, recruiting among, 201

D

Danger, in job profiles, 68
Deadlines, in job profiles, 68
Decision-making, in organizational culture, 209
Demonstrated capacities, 126
Development Dimensions
  International, 109
Dictionary of Occupational Titles,
  63-65
Disabilities, hiring people with,
  193-94
Discrimination
  in hiring, 189-91, 193-94
  in interviewing, 175-76
  in testing, 143-44
Disney Company, 20-22
Disposition, 41-42
Diversity, 204
Division of labor, 59-60
Domains, 46-47
Drucker, Peter, 34
Duration,
  in job profiling, 87-89
  of job tasks 69, 70

E

Educational/developmental
  capacity, 84-85
Emotional capacity, 79
Emotional rewards, 48-50, 191
Employee Reliability Inventory,

Employees
  assessing (*See* Assessments; Tests)
  as competitive advantage, 3-4
  diversity of, 204
  firing, 106-7
  labeling, 96-99
  matching with jobs, 5-8
  recruiting by, 198-99
  status in organizational culture, 210, 212
  temporary, 105, 106-7, 196
  turnover of, 5, 205-207
Employee selection. *See* Assessments; Hiring; Interviews
Employment law, 190-91
Employment testing. *See* Tests
Environmental capacity, 80
Equal Employment Opportunity Commission
  discrimination complaints to, 190-91
  job analysis standards of, 72
Equally qualified applicants, fallacy of, 23-24
Equipment, 213
Ethical capacity, 79-80
Exceptional factors, of job tasks, 68-69
Exclusionary rules, 28-32
Experience, 8, 21-23

F
Facial hair, in hiring policies, 21
Federal government. *See* U.S. government
Firings, 106-7
First impressions, 53-54, 100
Fiscal capacity, 86
Fit. *See* Job fit
Frequency,
  in job profiling, 87-89
  of job tasks, 69

G
Gardner, Howard, 113, 141, 146
General cognitive ability tests, 153-45
Greenberg, Herbert M., 6, 139-140, 160
Groups, candidate assessments by, 127-28, 180, 190

H
Halo effect, 160
Hiring
  casual approach to, 9-10
  costs of, 4-5, 8-10, 198
  discrimination in, 189-91
  key do's and don'ts, 192-93
  managers' ignorance about, 12-14
  Natural Selection Method described, 14-18
  and organizational priorities, 66
  people with disabilities, 193-94
  for productivity, 10-12
Honesty tests, 131
Human attributes
  critical, 23
  negative, 125, 127, 173, 183-84
  personal attitudes, 42-43
  rating scale for, 70-71
Human retrofitting, 5-8, 13
Hunter, John E., 4-5

I
IBM, 188-89
In-box test, 108
Industrial/organizational psychologists, 185
Industrial Revolution, 59-60
Industry-changers, 195-96
Influence capacity, 81
Information exchange, in organizational culture, 211, 213
Innovation, in organizational culture, 213
Institute of Management Consultants, 33

Integrity tests, 131
Intelligence tests, 28-29, 143-45, 143
Interest inventories, 139-40
Internal validity, 166-67
Internships, 201-2
Interpersonal capacity, 80-81
Interviews
  analyzing answers, 171-73
  behavior interviews, 155-58, 159-63
  flowchart for, 181
  multiple, 127-28, 180, 183
  on the job, 110-11
  overview of process, 180-85
  reliability and validity of, 174-77
  software for, 161-62
  time requirements of, 183, 184
  for values, 163-71
  See also Assessments
Intra-personal capacity, 80

J

Job descriptions
  differing views of, 61-62
  important elements of, 58, 61
  and profiling, 63, 65-70
Job evaluation, 63
Job fit
  and competence, 25-28
  and motivation, 50-52
  and personality, 43-44, 50-54
Job interviews. See Interviews
Job Profile Matrix
  for Natural Selection Hiring Method, 87, 88
  as source of assessment information, 117, 124
Jobs
  defined, 73-74
  differing views of, 61-62
  evaluating, 63
  key qualifications for, 115-22
  Labor Department categories, 63-65
  matching employees with, 5-8
  nature of, 59-61
  profiling, 63, 65-72, 87, 88
  (see also Performance domains)
Judgment scales, 125-26

K

Key Qualifications Profile, 117-22
Knowledge and abilities domain, 74, 83-86
KSAO model, 75-76

L

Labels, in assessment, 96-99
Labor, division of, 59-60
Labor Department, *Dictionary of Occupational Titles*, 63-65
Lawsuits, for discrimination, 175-77, 190-91
Lawyers, 191-92
Lee, Bill, 129
Leveler questions, 173-74
Liability characteristics, 125
Licenses. See Credentials
Lie detectors, 135
Life-long learning, 169-70
Losyk, Bob, 112

M

Magnet recruiting, 197-98
Major job functions, 67-68
Management education, 12-14
Management style, 209
Managers
  assessing, 108
  ignorance of sound hiring practices, 12-14
  retail, 5, 7-8
Mass production, 59-60
Maturity, 121, 156-57
McClelland, David C., 30-31
Mechanical capacity, 82
Meeting Professionals International, 33
Minimum qualifications, 28-32
Minorities, test bias against, 143-44 (*see also* Discrimination)

Misemployment, 5-8, 40
Mission, in organizational culture, 209
Mistakes, asking candidates about, 173-74
Money, versus emotional rewards, 51-52
Motivation
  assessing, 163-71
  and job fit, 42-44, 50-52
Multiple interviews, 127-28, 180, 183
Musical capacity, 86
Myers-Briggs Type Indicator, 97-98, 149

N
National Occupational Competency Testing Institute, 147
National Speakers Association, 33
Natural capacity, 86
Natural Selection Hiring Method
  goals of, 48
  interviewing flowchart for, 181
  introduction to, 14-18
  Job Profile Matrix for, 87, 88
  job profiling in, 63, 65-70
  performance domains in. *See* Performance domains
Negative attributes, 125
Numerical capacity, 84
Nurturing capacity, 82

O
Office of Strategic Services (OSS), 107-8
Older workers, recruiting, 199-200
O*NET, 64-65
On-the-job assessments, 102-103
Open houses, 193
Organizational culture
  attributes of, 208-13
  requirements of, 44, 52-53
Organizational priorities, 66, 208-13

Otwell, George, 36, 37
Outcomes, specifying, 66

P
Pay, and organizational culture, 212
Performance, labeling, 96-99
Performance domains
  applied to job analysis, 72-78
  categories of, 74
  knowledge and abilities, 74, 83-86
  performance processes, 74, 82-83
  personal, 74, 78-80
  relationships, 74, 80-82
Performance processes, 74, 82-83
Performance reviews, bias in, 31-32
Personal contact, differing needs for, 43, 45
Personal domain, 74, 78-80
Personality
  and competence, 96-99
  dominant, 45-46
  and job fit, 41-42, 48-52
  and performance, 23, 42-50
  relevance of, 39-42
  unacceptable, 125, 127, 173, 183-84
Personality profiles, 97-98, 140, 148-49
Personal values, 75
Physical capacity
  assessing, 119-20
  elements of, 80
Police officers, 28-30
Policies, consistent application of, 211
Political capacity, 81-82
Polygraphs, 135
Position Analysis Questionnaire, 62
Potential, and competence, 33-36, 75

220 Index

Practical capacity, 82-83
Predictive validity, 175. *See also* Tests; Validity
Prejudice, in interviews, 175-76, 177-80
Priorities
 of job tasks, 69
 organizational, 66, 201-6
Probationary period, 105-6
Probing questions, 93-94
Process orientation, 202
Productive fit, 8
Productivity, in employee selection, 4-5, 10-12
Professional associations, 33
Profiling of jobs, 63, 65-72, 87, 88
Profitability, and employee satisfaction, 207
Promotions, 7
Promus Hotels, 110
Psychic rewards, 50-52, 198
Psychological tests. *See* Tests
Psychologists, 185

Q

Qualifications
 versus competence, 20-22
 and credentials, 32-38
 defined, 20
 equal, 23-24
 establishing, 115-22
 and job experience, 6, 19-20
 minimum, 28-32

R

Racial discrimination, 142-44, 171-72, 189-90
Recruiting
 by employees, 198-99
 examples of, 195-97
 magnet, 197-98
 Techniques for, 198-205
 See also Assessments; Hiring; Interviews
References, 111-12, 121-22
Reid Psychological Systems, 148-49
Rejections, 127, 129
Relationship domain, 74, 80-82
Reliability
 of assessment tools, 94-96
 of interviews, 174-77
 of tests, 94-96, 137-38, 149-52
Represented competence, 103-104
Responsibility, assessing for, 121
Résumés, value of, 40-41
Retail clerks, competencies of, 49
Retention, factors in, 205-207
Retrofitting employees, 5-8, 13
Rewards, monetary vs. emotional, 50-52, 191
Rhoades, Ann, 110
Risk orientation, 210

S

Salaries, and organizational culture, 212
Sales representatives, needs of, 45-46
Samples, 103-104
Scenario questions, 158
Schmidt, Frank L., 4-5
Schools, recruiting in, 201-02
Schwarzenegger, Arnold, 26-28
Scrap and rework, turnover as, 17, 205
Sears, 131-32
Selection. *See* Hiring
Self-management capacity, 83
Sensory capacity, 84
Simulations, 107-10
Skill-fill fallacy, 20
Smart Hire software, 161-62
Social needs, 45
Society of Industrial and Organizational Psychology, 185
Soft skills, 23
Software, for interviewing, 161-62
Southwest Airlines, 189-90
Spatial/artistic capacity, 84
State employment agencies, 199

Status, in organizational culture, 210
Structure, needs for, 49-50, 100-101
Suitability, versus capability, 48-49

T
Teams, emergence of, 60-61
Teamwork
  and competence, 25-27
  in organizational culture, 210, 211
Technical capacity, 85-86
Technology, 109-10, 201
Temperament, and performance, 73
Temporary workers, 105, 203
Tests
  benefits of, 132-33
  deciding whether to use, 133-43
  and examinees' rights, 142-43
  intelligence, 30-31, 143-45
  misuse of, 138-40
  reliability and validity of, 94-96, 135-39, 149-52
  resistance to, 140-41, 146-47
  selected distributors of, 147-49
  types of, 102
  use by Sears, 131-32
  See also Assessments
Test takers' rights, 142-43
Time capacity, 83
Trade associations, 33
Travel, 68
Turnover, 5, 205-07

U
Uniform Guidelines on Employee Selection Procedures, 137
U.S. government
  Dictionary of Occupational Titles, 63-65
  job analysis standards of, 72
U.S. Office of Strategic Services, 107-8

V
Validity
  of assessment tools, 95-96
  internal, 166-67
  of interviews, 174-77
  of tests, 95-96, 137-39, 149-52
Values
  of job candidates, 75, 163-71
  in organizational culture, 202
Verbal capacity, 84
Virtual reality, 109-10

W
Web sites, recruiting on, 201
Welfare recipients, recruiting, 195, 199
Wiggins, Grant, 17, 102, 115, 122
Wonderlic Personnel Test, Inc., 145, 147-48
Work
  motivation for. *See* Motivation
  nature of, 59-61
  profiling, 61, 65-72, 87, 88
  See also Jobs; Performance domains
Work behaviors
  in Candidate Assessment Grid, 124
  defined, 75
  in Natural Selection Hiring Method, 79-86
  See also Behavior
Workers. *See* Employees
Workload, in organizational culture, 210, 211
Work product, 103-104
Work site
  interviews at, 110-11
  physical conditions of, 212
  tone of, 210
Work structure, differing needs for, 45-46, 100-101